Cultural Divide

Cultural Divide
A Study of African-American College-Level Writers

Valerie M. Balester

Boynton/Cook Publishers
HEINEMANN
Portsmouth, NH

Boynton/Cook Publishers, Inc.
A subsidiary of Reed Publishing (USA) Inc.
361 Hanover Street, Portsmouth, New Hampshire 03801
Offices and agents throughout the world

Editor: Robert W. Boynton
Production: Renee M. Pinard
Cover and text design: Tom Allen/Pear Graphic Design

The author would like to thank the following for permission to reprint
copyrighted material in this book:
Figure 2.1: From "Black Talking on the Streets" by Roger Abraham. In
Explorations in the Ethnography of Speaking, eds. R. Bauman and J.
Sherzer. Copyright © 1974. Reprinted by permission of Cambridge Uni-
versity Press.

Library of Congress Cataloging-in-Publication Data
Balester, Valerie M.
    Cultural divide : a study of African-American college-level writers
/ Valerie M. Balester.
      P. cm.
    ISBN 0-86709-325-0
    1. English language—Rhetoric—Study and teaching—Texas—
Austin—Case studies. 2. Afro-American college students—Texas—
Austin—Language—Case Studies. 3. Language and culture—Texas—
Austin—Case studies. 4. Black English—Texas—Austin—Case studies.
I. Title.
PE1405.U6B34   1993
427'.973'08996—dc20   93-18826
                                                                CIP

Printed in the United States of America on acid-free paper
97 96 95 94 93   BC   5 4 3 2 1

Contents

Foreword

One of the strongest threads of research and criticism in composition studies reveals the inherent consistency, the rhetorical integrity, even the brilliant folkways that emerge among students whom we have labeled "basic writers" (often as a way of predicting their failure). Drawing strength from linguistics, literary criticism, cognitive psychology, and cultural anthropology, scholars as sympathetic and wise as Mina Shaughnessy, Mike Rose, and Shirley Brice Heath have shown how students, reaching for the keys to success in school, invent ways of writing that, though inappropriate or incorrect according to academic norms, make perfect sense when we consider where the students have come from and how little they know about the academic world they enter in their drive for upward social mobility. What can we give to these students and what do they bring to us?

In this new book, Valerie Balester pursues answers to these questions as one of the new breed of teacher-researchers who examine students' work not only with the discerning eye of the grammarian but also with the tireless inquiry of the rhetorical critic and ethnographer. Combining the methods of sociolinguistics (close listening) with those of literary scholarship (close reading), Professor Balester pauses thoughtfully at the intersection of talk and writing. In crossing back and forth between orality and literacy, in interviews and in writing, in reading and listening, she opens a haven where her student-informants can express and explore the full range of their linguistic options, where the springs of identity meet the mainstream of academic discourse. The result is a subtly designed study that challenges the narrow imposition of stylistic norms in composition classes, that urges a more critical and open approach to the teaching of college writing, and that questions the limits of our supposed commitment to diversity in education.

The study has an interesting twist: Instead of focusing on the struggles of basic writers, in the manner of Shaughnessy and Rose, Professor Balester treats the work of students who, in varying degrees, have "made it," who have crossed the cultural divide between life in a second-dialect minority and the life of the educated classes represented by the American university. In retracing the course of their journeys, Balester shows how these good students have adapted the resources they bring with them to the tasks that lie before them. We learn as much about what they have lost as about what they have gained; we see what they feel forced to relinquish as they stride toward what they hope to achieve.

The book thus touches upon a sensitive topic—the fate of African-American discourse among successful, educated blacks. Whereas many composition researchers have dealt with the problems of second-dialect students, none that I know of has drawn as deeply as Professor Balester upon the rich literature describing the practices of black rhetoric in the street, the home, the pulpit, and the poem to discover how students seek to compensate for their lack of academic eloquence by depending on more familiar forms of eloquence, such as "fancy talk" and "signifying." The more conscious they become of these strategies, however, the more likely the students are to feel ambivalent about their rhetorical heritage and to doubt its appropriateness and effectiveness in the wide white world of education and commerce. While in other studies black students are obliged to appear as victims of an educational system that beckons to them, only finally to reject them as unfit, this new study suggests that what is endangered is not always the students themselves, but their rhetorical inventiveness and their identity with the discourse communities from which they emerge.

Confronted with the prospect of linguistic diversity, many readers of this book will grow wary, remembering the simplistic relativism of the early manifesto *Students' Right to Their Own Language*. But, in the context of new demands for diversity and multicultural education, it is time for us to consider anew the consequences of our efforts to instill our own rhetorical values in our students. This task inevitably confronts the much discussed issue of "political correctness," especially as it centers on the general public's increasing realization of a premise English teachers have always accepted: *Language really does make a difference*. Words are not merely the vehicles of thought and information; sentences and stories are not just substitutes for action. With every word we speak, we reveal ourselves, and self-revelation is an act of great consequence in a world striving toward democracy.

Even a settled commitment to "education for all" leaves us, then, with the problem of our differences—different selves, different speech acts, different discourse paths. As Prentice Baptiste has said of multicultural education, the time for the language of inclusion has come—and gone; now the time arrives for the language of *critique*. Valerie Balester meets this challenge with timely observations on the interplay of discourse and character in the process by which young African-Americans are educated. With insight and creativity, she performs the positive service that Kant said accompanies the negative police-action of the best criticism: It stands against the violence that would prohibit each citizen from pursuing a vocation in freedom and peace.[1]

M. Jimmie Killingsworth
Director of Writing Programs
Texas A & M University

Notes

[1]The references in the last paragraph come from the following: Rosalind Alexander-Kasparik, Interview with Prentice Baptiste, University of Houston, quoted in "'To Weave a Stronger Cloth': Restructuring Schools to Build Strength in Diversity," *Sedletter* (Newsletter of the Southwest Educational Development Laboratory, Austin, Texas), January 1993, p. 4 and Immanuel Kant, *Critique of Pure Reason,* Trans. Norman Kemp Smith (New York: St. Martin's, 1965), p. 27.

Preface

My aim in this book is to show how some bidialectal African-American students face special problems in learning academic writing. Their problems are unique because they draw upon rhetorical strategies that baffle their teachers, with their mainstream expectations, but that nevertheless have a logic of their own, an internal consistency grounded in a variety of nonacademic, usually oral, traditions of discourse. My method is rhetorical criticism of students' texts, both written and spoken; I have taken great care to inform my analyses by consulting at length available research on African-American language and rhetoric.

Because of the interdisciplinary nature of this work, I have a variety of debts. I rest many basic assumptions on the theories of sociologists of knowledge. I am especially indebted to the work of Berger and Luckman, who have described the social construction of the reality of everyday life, including the way communities produce and maintain knowledge through language. I also wish to acknowledge the influence of R. B. Le Page and Andrée Tabouret-Keller, whose *Acts of Identity* provides one of the few extensively researched discussions of how speakers use language to assume an ethos, by modeling their style of speaking on their stereotyped conceptions of the groups with which they wish to be identified. An even greater influence has been sociologist Erving Goffman, who offers in *The Presentation of Self in Everyday Life* a primary model for the social construction of the self and, consequently, of ethos.

Reading Goffman, I am struck by how well the concept of self-construction applies to these students, whom I observe in the act of creating for themselves an ethos, or in Goffman's terms, a front. Yet I also realize that my perceptions must be colored by my own construction of personal reality. I myself am constructing an ethos for each subject as I read or listen. Surely my idea of young African-Americans influences my interpretations. Acknowledging my own prejudices (as a white, middle-class, female academic) reinforces my sense that rhetorical ethos, or the image of the speaker's or writer's character as presented through discourse, is vital to the success of any student who is not in the mainstream of academic culture. Since Black English Vernacular (BEV) speakers are not only newcomers to this culture, but also come from an alien, often despised and misunderstood language background, they must be at even greater pains than their more traditional classmates to demonstrate their good sense, good character, and good will—the components of effective rhetorical ethos. Merely to give off the image of the "good man, speaking well," as Cicero and Quintilian advocate, is not possible for students with major cultural differences from mainstream (mostly white, middle-class, male-dominated) society, which constitutes the American educational system.

I must also acknowledge the influence of the numerous scholars who have studied Black English Vernacular, including, among others, Dillard, Labov, Baugh, Mitchell-Kernan, Heath, and Kochman. Special mention should be made of Roger Abrahams' and Henry Louis Gates' studies on African-American rhetoric and speech acts.

On a more personal level, I want to thank those people who have made this book possible and who have encouraged me to pursue this work. I cannot name them all here, but I want to acknowledge the help of those most directly involved. For the infelicities and errors that remain in spite of their good advice I am fully responsible.

For assistance on the earliest version of this study, I am indebted to Lester Faigley, James Kinneavy, John Ruszkiewicz, and John Baugh. A special thanks to Ian Hancock for his encouragement and for his insight into language and identity.

For many hours of reading of the manuscript and for many hours of conversation, I thank Jimmie Killingsworth, Barbara Johnstone, Robert Boenig, Guy Bailey, Medhat Rabie, and Keith Walters. Those who read and evaluated Max's and Shanique's essays deserve special mention: John Slatin, Yvonne Kay Halasek, Nancy Peterson, Wayne Butler, and Jerome Bump.

I owe my family much gratitude, especially my parents, Fred Balester and Alison McLeod-Sharpe Balester, for encouragement and support. My brother, Marc Balester, listened to many hours of tapes and read the very first draft of the very first chapter of this book. My husband, Spiros Vellas, has proved his faith in me time and time again.

Most of all I thank those anonymous students, Max, Shanique, Laurie, Dinese, Divinity, Polo, Spike, and Thomas, whose cooperation meant everything to this book.

Notes

[1]Throughout this book I will use the acronym BEV to refer to Black English Vernacular and the acronym SAE to refer to Standard American English, what sociolinguist J. Fishman has called the language of "wider communication."

Introduction

American higher education is characterized by diversity. Students bring to the community college, the junior college, and the university an array of religious, ethnic, and racial backgrounds. Gradually, we are learning to value the experiences of those whose voices and knowledge have not shaped academic institutions or discourses—the experiences of minority students, of women students, of working-class students. Far from passively accepting the status quo, many of these students are themselves questioning institutional academic authority, listening to the voices of their cultures, and recognizing that their differences can be more than deficiencies. In places of higher education, many of us are taking note of diversity. But we are not always clear about what diversity means, about how, in terms of behavior, tradition, and language, we differ from one another.

This book is an attempt to understand some of those differences in regards to language, particularly writing, and thus to lay the groundwork for bridging the cultural divide between many composition teachers and their students. I see the building of bridges as a two-way process. We can start by helping students accommodate to traditional academic discourse. To achieve this, we may need to employ some new methods—methods based upon an analysis of the language and rhetoric with which culturally diverse students begin. Once we understand where they are coming from, we will find it easier to help them achieve their writing goals. There is another part of the process, however: The advantage will not be theirs alone. If we really explore and understand the language and rhetoric of diverse cultures, if we expose ourselves and all of our students to new forms of expression and new modes of communication, we will undoubtedly enrich the way we—as academics—write. In some small way, we may see academic discourses begin to accommodate to culturally diverse students.

I begin with African-American language and rhetoric, that is, with the vernacular used widely by African-Americans in many contexts. It is an appropriate starting place because decades of scholarly work prepare the way. More important, the need for a

1

better understanding of African-American rhetoric is pressing. Study after study shows a deplorable set of negative attitudes towards what literary, sociolinguistic, and anthropological scholarship has recognized as a truly vibrant and functional rhetorical tradition. Despite such recognition, the language of African-Americans is all too frequently judged uneducated, sloppy, and ugly, or believed to be a debased form of so-called correct English, with no discernible rules of grammar or use (Canuteson; Fraser; Kerr-Mattox; Piché, Rubin, et al; Seligman, Tucker, and Lambert; Shuy, Fasold, and Williams; Sonntag and Pool; Tucker and Lambert; Williams).

Such an attitude is counterproductive to learning, not to mention unfounded. And since identity is always intertwined with language, it can be downright damaging. For many African-Americans, Black English Vernacular, along with the rhetoric associated with it, has positive cultural associations (Garner and Rubin; Mays). Yet many others are torn between this positive attitude that recognizes and values BEV as a legitimate dialect with a respectable history and its opposite that sees BEV as a degrading mark of inferiority. Sadly, African-American students are often as unaware of their linguistic heritage as any of us and thus are less able to combat unfair and harmful estimations of it.

While scholarship on BEV has taught us much about this tradition, there remains much we do not know. Scholarship has concentrated for the most part on spoken language (especially Abrahams; Baugh; Hancock; Kochman; Labov; Mitchell-Kernan) because BEV is an oral not a written dialect. Some work on student writing has been done, but it generally deals with elementary/secondary level or underprepared college level students (Bentley; Heath; Scott). So far, we have paid scant attention to the average or superior college student. My point is that we can learn a great deal by attending to the texts of *successful* African-American college-level writers.

To this end, I have collected written and spoken texts from eight BEV-speaking African-American students who attended The University of Texas at Austin in 1987. The students were first- and second-year when I asked them to allow me to tape interviews with them and to provide me with samples of their writing. Their texts reveal writers attempting to construct a scholarly identity which, as novices, they had not yet fully assumed, and to address audiences of whom they as yet had little knowledge. In both their texts and in their interviews, they provide a fascinating source of insight into the unique talents and troubles of African-American college students.

The eight students who assisted me in this endeavor gave themselves pseudonyms at my suggestion. There were four females, Shanique, Laurie, Divinity, and Dinese, and four males, Max, Polo, Spike, and Thomas. Although when I collected the texts none were my students, I had taught Shanique, Laurie, and Max the previous summer. This acquaintance led me to ask Shanique and Max to be my "assistants" as well as informants in my study of what we called "Black English." They helped me recruit the other informants. All were paid five dollars an hour and were asked to sign consent forms and to provide some information about their backgrounds and attitudes toward BEV.

I decided to collect both spoken and written texts, because BEV is an oral dialect and because speech and writing interact dynamically, as researchers have noted with increasing frequency (Britton; Kroll and Vann; Olson). All interviews were taped, and all writing was timed. To make my samples cover as wide a range as possible yet allow for comparisons, I collected a range of styles from careful to casual in both the written and spoken modes, often on the same topic in each mode.

Thus, to elicit casual spoken discourse, I had Shanique interview the females and Max the males, giving them free range of topics. For casual written discourse, I asked each informant to write a letter to a friend of the same gender, and, as I had informed them I would, I made a photocopy for analysis and mailed the original. To elicit more careful discourse, I interviewed the students myself. I asked for personal stories to encourage narrative and for opinions to encourage persuasive discourse. I also asked students to write narrative and persuasive essays, arranging the interview and essay prompts so that each would write and speak on the same topic at least once. In some cases, they wrote first and interviewed later, and in other cases the reverse was true.

What emerged from this mass of data were not simply static texts for analysis but complex attitudes toward BEV (outlined in Chapter 1) and a glimpse into rhetoric in action. Attitudes expressed toward BEV were often ambivalent. While the informants all recognized BEV as a powerful component of African-

American culture and a source of solidarity, a number of them also devalued it as "improper."

Their awareness that BEV and BEV speakers are often judged as deficient contributed, no doubt, to the high sense of ethos that emerged in their texts. These were writers who were acutely aware of how they would be perceived by me and by eventual readers of my research. Thus they always constructed their ethos to influence the possible prejudices of multiple audiences—especially to me as a researcher/teacher, who eavesdropped even on their conversations with each other and their personal letters, and to the educated readers they assumed I would eventually address. In constructing ethos, they performed an intricate balancing act, suiting their personas not only to the multiple audiences but also to each of their own various roles as researchers, informants, African-Americans, and college students. Their attempt to control ethos, to appear as members in good standing of the academic discourse community, resulted in their use of or rejection of a number of African-American rhetorical strategies. (Chapter 2 gives an overview of African-American rhetoric.) For example, in Chapter 3 I describe how the informants use "signifying," an indirect and thus polite way of commenting on another's behavior, to distance themselves from the research. By this means, they protect themselves from facile labeling and gain some measure of control over how they will be perceived.

In Chapters 4 and 6, I describe some other African-American rhetorical strategies which, with differing results, the informants brought to their writing. In approximating academic discourse, Max, Polo, and Thomas all apparently draw on African-American preaching and prayer traditions as well as on an elaborate style called fancy talk, both of which are associated with formal and intellectual rhetoric. Laurie, in an apparent attempt to sound lady-like, draws upon the African-American tradition of respectable talk, employing many superpolite forms in both speech and writing. Unfortunately in all these cases there is great potential for misreading on the part of composition teachers. Fancy talk may be seen as inflated boasting, while respectable talk may be seen as powerless and indecisive.

In Chapter 5, we see how proscriptions against BEV in academic prose can adversely affect student writing. In oral storytelling, Shanique constructs an independent and spirited ethos, in the

African-American tradition of the smart talker, by drawing on the covert prestige of BEV. Her sense that she cannot use BEV in an academic narrative leaves her without alternatives for constructing this witty and effective ethos in writing.

As the texts of these informants make abundantly clear, African-American students bring a substantial linguistic and rhetorical sophistication to their writing. This is a source of expressive and intellectual power that composition teachers have failed to tap, yet students like Max and Shanique and the other informants find ways on their own to adjust to the demands of college writing. Perhaps their contribution to this study will help bridge the cultural divide by creating for future students, for African-Americans and others who represent diversity, a climate of greater understanding and acceptance of their unique linguistic and rhetorical heritage. I am sure they hoped it would.

Attitudes and Expectations

Becoming a college writer is tantamount to undergoing an initiation in the academy's ways with words.[1] Although all students must adjust their dialects and understanding of written language to meet unfamiliar academic standards and conventions, African-American students are at a disadvantage in this initiation process because of cultural difference. The same can be said of any students from a culture substantially distinguishable from the white, middle-class mainstream. The more discrimination or prejudice that exists against them or their culture, the greater their problems. Not only is assimilation more difficult, but it may require disassociation from the primary culture (Heath, *Ways with Words;* Fordham and Ogbu; Fordham; Fine; Sonntag and Pool). Heath has amply demonstrated that literacy is affected by culture. She observed that children in the Carolina Piedmont reared in homes significantly different in culture from those of the white middle class majority, which controlled the schools, had more difficulty adjusting to school norms and expectations. For the most part, neither teachers nor parents recognized the cultural reasons for the children's failure, attributing it most often to their lack of ability or to the teachers' lack of skill (Heath, *Ways with Words*).

Only those students who had fairly successfully adjusted to school could survive at The University of Texas at Austin in 1986–1987. As freshmen, Max, Shanique, and their friends had new adjustments to make, adjustments that were in some ways similar to those of every college student but in other ways unique. Their Anglo or Hispanic peers did not possess their knowledge of BEV and African-American rhetoric.

There have been so many claims about BEV, so many opinions about it, so many teachers and parents and school districts encouraging it or working to eradicate it, that the average African-American is bound to have some opinions about it. Although the terms *Black English* and *BEV* or its variants were unfamiliar to all my informants, they revealed sophistication in their ability to reflect on the topic and great interest in language. In fact, they often insisted on turning our conversation to this topic which so touched their lives.

They knew all too well, I surmise, that they had been and would be judged on their language, that BEV could be a blight as well as a blessing. Usually they expressed ambivalence toward BEV. So Max, in his essay on Black English, calls for a blend of BEV and Standard American English (SAE)—preserving the best but eradicating the worst of both dialects—rather than a separate but equal coexistence:

> The question that exist in the annals of my mind now is, When will we reach that golden day when color will no longer be a factor, when speech will be a unified body in America as well as unity amongst all races, and when Black and white English will no longer represent a seperate Black and White world and will be associated with a peaceful united term Whack English?[2]

Sadly, his portmanteau word could as easily have been "Blite" as "Whack." Equally anomalous and impossible, the former connotes sickness and drought, the latter, comedy (wacky).

In this same essay, Max acknowledges that racism lies behind attitudes toward BEV, that people expect him, because of his race, to be inept with language:

> Though I did not grow up in a ghetto, as a Black youth I have been crippled by societies ghetto mentality. This mentality stereotypes me too as unfit to make it in a properly unbroken English spoken world. I have been educated and have realized that my writing is a tool to express feelings otherwise hushed or shuned by society. Poetry being many Black's ticket to open protest, I have compassed an outright, however limited view of the moral debasement and silent awakening of the Black race.

Max displays ambivalence toward BEV in this passage: he associates it with a lack of education and with unjust limitations placed on African-Americans. Yet while BEV is the language of the ignorant, it is black, being the unique language of a people, with a poetry of its own, and thus Max accords it some prestige.

The Drawbacks: BEV As Blight

Sociolinguistic studies indicate that Max is justified in his charge of being stereotyped as unable to speak "properly." BEV is apparently negatively viewed by the majority of teachers, whatever their ethnicity. Much of the work on language attitudes has been done in Texas, which is fortunate since it gives at least some sense of what the educational situation was like for Max and his friends. It is probable that attitudes found in Texas are common elsewhere in the United States. In a recent survey at Texas A & M University of 132 students in graduate education classes, all former or current teachers, and of 244 undergraduate education majors, Beverly Kerr-Mattox found negative attitudes toward BEV deeply entrenched. Among her respondents were six African-Americans, twenty-four Hispanics, and eight Asian Americans. Respondents listened to tapes of middle school children of different ethnic backgrounds and were asked to decide what occupation would best suit the speakers. For the most part they designated occupations such as factory worker or cashier for the BEV speakers. While Kerr-Mattox's survey is somewhat limited in scope, it points to a problem in image for BEV speakers.

In 1982, Mary Alice Canuteson surveyed English teachers and language arts supervisors in Texas on their perceptions of BEV and concluded that their attitudes could be characterized as negative and were manifested by a desire to eradicate the use of BEV in the schools. She noted that "The educational force in Texas does not know enough about [vernacular black English] to deal effectively with black dialect speakers" and that necessary "training in the language and culture of the black English speakers . . . for those who teach that segment of school society . . . is not supported by the teachers or supervisors" (abstract).[3]

BEV speakers learning to read or write get negative messages about their abilities both because of the way they speak and because of their race. Their problems are probably compounded if, as emerging bidialectals, their writing shows evidence of unmistakable BEV features or if in reading aloud they translate the SAE of their school books back into BEV. Although we can presently only speculate on the effects of such a negative image, it is obvious that it stereotypes students and probable that it creates obstacles to learning. It almost certainly creates conflicts in identity, and for many BEV speakers affects self-esteem. It also contributes to linguistic insecurity, the sense that everything one says is subject to censure. Such insecurity leads to a process of constant monitoring in situations where careful language is expected. The speaker monitors his or her speech to approximate the standard, which can lead to hypercorrection, whereby a grammatical rule is imperfectly applied or overgeneralized (as when "goed" is used for "went"). It is less frequently realized that monitoring can occur as well in situations where nonstandard speech is appropriate and can result in a hyper, or exaggerated, version of BEV (Mitchell-Kernan *Language Behavior*, 60).

A study by Fine in 1987 notes that negative valuation of BEV creates as much dissonance for successful urban students as for their unsuccessful peers. Clearly, successful students pay a price by conforming to school culture and language. School is associated with white culture and thus is recognized as an instrument of social control and oppression. School does not always provide an escape from racism but rather serves a gatekeeping function to keep minorities in place. Successful students may be ostracized by peers (in one New York school they are labeled "brainiacs") for thinking they are better than others, for "acting white," in essence, for their disloyalty to the larger, dominant group at the expense of the vernacular culture (Fordham; Fordham and Ogbu). However, there is no evidence that African-American adults stigmatize academic success.

Survival strategies are adopted by successful students that enable them to do well academically while simultaneously retaining the goodwill of their peers. Certainly the effort of applying these strategies detracts from students' ability to perform well, but many do well enough to get by, and others excel in spite of the odds against them. Perhaps the most interesting of the strategies is what Fordham calls "racelessness," whereby students develop a persona that denies cultural difference. They strongly adopt the dominant ideology that equal opportunity is available for all who are deserving. In doing so, they reject the African-American cultural emphasis on cooperation and group identity and thus often suffer from a sense of conflict and ambivalence about their allegiance. By choosing racelessness, they declare themselves neither African-American nor white, neither bound nor advantaged by race.

One way students can exhibit racelessness is through a rejection of BEV. It is clear to anyone that schools discourage and devalue BEV. It is equally clear that students are rewarded (by the school) for rejecting BEV. By the same token, students who speak only SAE are subject to the harassment of their peers, which can be nothing short of brutal in elementary and high school. Because they have opted for a variety of language associated with the white world, they are seen as violating solidarity and shared norms of social identity (Mitchell-Kernan *Language Behavior*, 77).

Rachel L. Jones, while a sophomore at Southern Illinois University, wrote an essay that rebels against the equation of standard English and race. By her own testimony, she suffered for her standard English:

> The first time it happened to me I was nine years old. Cornered in the school bathroom by the class bully and her sidekick, I was offered the opportunity to swallow a few of my teeth unless I satisfactorily explained why I always got good grades, why I talked "proper" or "white." I had no ready answer for her, save the fact that my mother had from the time I was old enough to talk stressed the importance of reading and learning, or that L. Frank Baum and Ray Bradbury were my closest companions. I somehow talked my way out of a beating.

However, Rachel is not obviously on one side or another in this conflict. The article shows a decided ambivalence. She admits that "it is almost Jekyll and Hyde-ish the way I can slip out of academic abstractions into a long, lean, double-negative filled dialogue" in the proper context, with family and friends. Yet she also rails against Labov's suggestion that having command of both dialects might be advantageous, and she argues that BEV will keep African-Americans oppressed because it "excludes them from full participation in the world we live in." Is she suggesting that BEV be eradicated? Or simply that African-Americans stop stigmatizing SAE? She does not argue that the dominant culture stop stigmatizing BEV but puts the burden of change on her peers.

In a study of middle class African-American attorneys, Garner and Rubin found the same strategy for coping with identity conflicts. They conclude that "successful blacks . . . disassociate S[tandard] E[nglish] from cultural identification with white America, thus enabling them to adopt the prestige speech variety without embracing a frequently antagonistic culture" (46). Like Rachel

Jones, who ends her essay by claiming "I don't think I talk white, I think I talk right," these attorneys equate SAE with educated speech. They also attach high prestige to BEV and use it themselves in what they perceive as the right contexts. Yet, like Rachel Jones (who notes almost indignantly that James Baldwin "even went so far as to label [BEV] a language in its own right") they do not go so far as to accord BEV status as a dialect or language.

Sadly, all of the eight informants in this study show some degree of negative feeling toward BEV, based on its association with "bad" or "improper" or "uneducated" English. They express the belief that standard English is the "correct" dialect and that deviations from the standard represent error and ignorance. At the same time, they indicate that BEV can be useful or even beautiful. And a few of them define BEV by lexicon alone so that they can preserve the distinctive slang and condemn the improper grammar. In this model, BEV is denoted simply as *slang* or *slangs*. Slang is thought of as occurring almost exclusively on the level of lexicon—but in practice, no one speaking it would use formal or semi-formal standards for grammar and sprinkle in BEV words. Garner and Rubin found the same attitudes: "Informants mostly defined B[lack] E[nglish] as lack of grammatical rules and structure" yet they "held the expressiveness of B[lack] E[nglish] in high regard." They "felt that the 'slang' aspect of B[lack] E[nglish] was its most positive quality," and they characterized slang by lexicon and by "rhythm" (42).

In this regard Labov mentions covert prestige, whereby certain positive traits are associated with the minority dialect (*Sociolinguistic Patterns* 310–14). Students' attitudes may actually be more positive than many realize. Luberta Mays studied black children's attitudes toward their nonstandard speech in a school setting. In spite of frequent negative attitudes on the part of teachers, the children did not perceive their speech as "bad."

An example of this sort of thinking is offered by Max's friend Polo, who believes that BEV is "uneducated" and that SAE is "proper." He expresses understanding of blacks' use of BEV even though he feels it keeps them down:

> I [am] not quite sure what Black English is defined as. I do realize that most uneducated blacks speak what is defined to be slang terms but most people put blacks down for speaking this way, and I don't think it's truly our fault because we had to learn a new language and

in the course of learning English either we weren't taught well or we had to improvise or put words in because of lack of knowledge of the "proper" English.

Polo is defensive; while he displays sophisticated knowledge of language issues (note how he puts "proper" in quotes in this written opinion), he seems bent on making the point that blacks can speak as "properly" as anyone.

Like Polo, Dinese is defensive. She writes: "A lot of people associate ungrammatical English with 'Black English,' but even with my father's family (from country Mississippy) we had to speak with correct structure. Nevertheless, it still sounds 'Black.'" She asserts that African-Americans can speak just as "properly" as anyone, even when they may be considered "hick." At the same time, she implies that there is nothing wrong with sounding "black," that BEV is a matter of pronunciation and maybe lexicon but not structure (i.e., grammar).

All of the informants use the term *proper* to describe grammatically correct language, while *intellectual* seems to convey not only correctness but something beyond, something that creates that "intellectual air" and that uses the "big" words characteristic of some forms of African-American rhetoric (particularly *fancy* or *sweet talk*, discussed in Chapter 2). Anyone with a certain level of education can talk proper, but it takes real wit to talk intellectual.

In my interview of him, Polo makes an explicit connection between the use of big words and sounding intellectual:

> My school's half white, half black, therefore I was exposed to, you know, speaking more Standard English . . . and . . . I was also put in a situation where I had to watch . . . because, you know, I was in many academic contests. But most blacks that, you know, they just in the neighborhood and . . . they're not necessarily academically oriented, so they don't see any need to be trying to, to say all that big words, as they call it, you know, [changes voice to imitate them] "Don't be saying all those big words."

As Polo indicates, talking intellectual is an achievement that sets one apart from the average. Notice that his comment shows that he correlates talking intellectual with SAE. In his opinion, one cannot talk intellectual in BEV, although by the same token talking SAE does not of itself constitute talking intellectual. He also indicates that big words are an important feature of talking intellectual.

Polo frequently uses the terms *talking intellectual* and *proper.* His comments show remarkable sophistication and attention to language:

> See actually, I've learned that in order to succeed in this world there's a certain way you have to talk, in certain situations I must talk in that manner. That's why I decided I was not going to use double negatives and things, ain't and things like that. It wasn't because I . . . didn't like the way I was speaking. It was because I realized that if I did talk that way I would . . . be looked down upon or have lesser intelligence.

At first glance he seems to be saying that BEV grammar is acceptable but different. He recognizes the social handicap of using it in the wrong situations. However, his attitude is ambivalent. He goes on to argue that "poor, uneducated whites" and "poor, uneducated blacks" speak the same: "As far as using ain't and improper language, that's universal." Like Max, he calls BEV grammar "improper." He carefully relates this improper grammar to economic class rather than to race. Middle class blacks mostly talk proper, unless they are in conversation with their lower class counterparts, because, like Polo himself, "Mostly intellectual blacks just realize that they need to speak proper if they want to succeed." In other words, they learn not a new dialect (SAE) but the *right way* to talk, the way school teaches. At the same time he uses *proper* to designate correct grammar, Polo shows sensitivity to the situational nature of language: "I think because some blacks when they're speaking Black English they use improper English. They use ain't and stuff and then that just makes the whole thing sound bad to *some* people." In this comment he seems to avoid condemning the way the lower class people speak (with, as he puts it, double negatives and "ain't"). Still, he expresses clearly his sense that such language leaves a taint in the eyes of some people, presumably educated and upper class people. To summarize, Polo seems sometimes to mean correct English by the term *proper*, that is SAE used without regard to the situation, and at other times to mean SAE used in appropriate settings for particular purposes.

He may be struggling to make sense of his conflicting negative and positive attitudes toward BEV. An ethnographic study of an

African-American teacher at a community college in a large north-eastern city reports awareness of this conflict. The teacher, Ms. Morris, whose own teaching style is influenced by the African-American homiletic tradition, maintains that "schooling weakens the Black community by teaching 'successful' students to break their ties to the community by rejecting its behavior, norms, and values." She is quoted directly, from a taped interview: "[Y]ou know how some Black folks are once they get education right, they get a superiority attitude. 'Nigger, I got mine, you gotta get yours the best way you can cause I'm Black and I done made it and I ain't gonna be bothered with you, you're trash'" (Foster 24). John Edgar Wideman, noted African-American novelist, writing about himself, reveals a similar awareness:

> I was running away from Pittsburgh, from poverty, from blackness. To get ahead, to make something of myself, college had seemed a logical, necessary step; my exile, my flight from home began with good grades, with good English, with setting myself apart long before I'd earned a scholarship and a train ticket over the mountains to Philadelphia. (26–27)

The BEV speaker is always torn between double voices; the educated SAE brings benefits while it alienates from BEV, and the familiar, homey BEV brings scorn while it establishes solidarity and allows for greater expressiveness. Even those who ridicule SAE speakers and chastise them for "acting white" are aware of this problem and are often willing to concede that "proper" English has value—as long as it is seen as belonging to everyone, not just whites.

In another instance Polo demonstrates an ambivalent attitude toward BEV by a distinction between talking intellectual and talking proper:

Polo: You can talk proper and then you can talk intellectual. . . . Now I could talk to my black friends I'm saying, well, you know, using all these big words, you know, intellectually oriented, "This irked me," and such and such, but I don't talk like that cause that takes an effort, not a effort but when you talk intellectually you're using the thought process in what you're saying . . . so that everything can, uh, be cohesive . . . but, when, you know, when I talk to my black friends I don't use, I don't use ain't and I do not use double negatives, so I, I try not to, you know, I know I do . . . but I try not to. And my close black friends are the ones I . . . correct them . . . it's like, "Man," . . . they say, . . . "Hey, you got to realize that you gonna have to learn to speak Standard English," and . . . now they appreciate it. . . But it's hard for 'em . . . like most times they'll . . . say, "Man, I'm not gonna do nothing today." And I say, "I'm doing what?" And I say, well, I repeat, I say, "You're not going to do nothing?" and, you know, then they see how it sounds . . .and once someone, you hear someone else say something that you pick it up quick . . . . And . . . when I say that, you know, "I'm not going to do anything" and . . . I speak like that where, wherever I'm at. It's just that, I don't,

Valerie: Is that so you can get the practice or because you just think that's the right way to talk?

Polo: I don't necessarily think it's the right way to talk, you know, a certain right way to talk. I just believe that that's the way it's most accepted.

In spite of the fact that Polo does not believe that BEV is inherently wrong, he is clearly, and rightly, convinced that it is socially (not linguistically) a handicap. His use of the term improper also suggests that he feels that in some senses it is indeed the wrong way to talk.

Polo's ambivalence reflects the dilemma of the BEV speaker who has been educated in the tradition that recognizes only one correct English, the formal standard, often in its written variety. He cannot totally reject BEV, the language he had to train himself to avoid, because it is also the language of his neighborhood and of many of his friends. And, although his writing and, when he speaks, his diction, display few hints of his first dialect, his pronunciation makes it clear that he is a BEV speaker, so that if he should slip into a BEV feature, as when he says "a effort" above, many listeners will be quick to relegate him to the class of the uneducated. He is well aware of this danger, and he takes pains to avoid it, but he is not willing to condemn himself or BEV completely. His dilemma is reflected again in the informants' distinction between "bad" English (i.e., ungrammatical and lacking prestige) and BEV. They associate BEV exclusively with slang. In other words, they define BEV solely in terms of lexicon. BEV grammatical and phonological forms are considered "bad" grammar. Bad grammar is a constant because the rules of grammar, learned in school as correct English, never change. In order to salvage BEV from being considered bad, then, it is necessary for them to define it as slang. Slang is good—it is colorful, homey, and familiar, and it promotes solidarity and a sense of identity. As

I will explain in more detail in Chapter 2, the folk term for talking bad often simply indicates the use of the nonstandard vernacular, without particular association with incorrect language. However, it seems also, especially for those involved in improving themselves through education, to carry further negative associations because it is being held up to a supposedly correct standard.

Opposed to talking proper, then, is *talking bad*. Max describes a friend of his who talks bad, although he does not explicitly use that term:

Max: I know a young lady who, I mean, she'll just talk and everything's backwards and mixed up, who attends this University, and, you know, I find myself, "Oh? Well you mean such and such and such" . . . And then, it's "Well, didn't I say that?" You know, but it's backwards, "She be is" and just slips . . . because she's so used to, uh, speaking a certain way that it becomes habit and, uh, you don't really notice what you're doing.

He betrays his own prejudice against BEV grammar when he imitates it by saying—"she be is"—which hardly resembles any legitimate BEV form. In fact, it is an example of hyper BEV (Mitchell-Kernan, *Language Behavior*, 60).

While BEV is not the correct medium for *intellectual talk*, it is the medium to create a sense of familiarity and solidarity, as Max indicates in talking to Thomas:

And I found that even in talking, you talking to me, you know, sometimes, you know, we can get black with each other, but then we can talk intellectual, also. But because of the mentality of us being black, I find that you know, you find yourself more, or most of the time, relating to me in black dialect.

Ironically, in this semi-formal situation at least, Max and Thomas speak very little BEV. It is possible that in a situation that was truly informal they would speak more of it, but given Thomas's very low opinion of BEV and the fact that both of them are in an environment where fluency in SAE is far more valued, it is unlikely.

They do point out that BEV is valued among certain African-American campus groups as a way to show solidarity, a fact which is quite annoying to Thomas, who claims he had to learn BEV as a second dialect in order to get along with his African-American peers. He believes Black English is a "joke" in which he must participate in order to speak informally with other African-Americans. His opinion of Black English is low indeed: "I don't feel it's really a language," he told me. He sees African-Americans as speaking either Black English, which is incorrect, or SAE, the language of the educated. He does not recognize that they might legitimately shift between dialects to accommodate to the situation. He seems to see such shifts as insincere. One should talk properly (if one is able). As he tells Max:

> Not every person who is black can actually go intellectually and speak with a Standard English that is, really is, the King's English and proper and all that, and actually use the words that constitute proper English. And phrases and all that kind of thing. There are not that many blacks here who are, you know, below average but . . . there are a few, and . . . it seems like even a lot of the intellectual ones that I've met like to go to Black English as compared to Standard English when communicating with other blacks. And it's hard. Because I don't always want to do that. I don't like to at all. But it's just I'm being kind of force fed the idea because I'm mingling with blacks, and . . . if I come off where there's fifty people speaking Black English and I'm trying to speak Standard English that, you know, is naturally just going to be a lot of misunderstanding about what I'm trying to do to them and what I'm trying not to be and I just don't want to . . . fight it anymore.

Thomas is frustrated by the fact that to show solidarity with other African-Americans and to show black identity he must speak a dialect he looks down upon. He seems so intent upon creating an intellectual ethos that he cannot even accept the others' limited definition of BEV as slang. For Thomas, even slang is improper.

Yet Thomas can and does speak BEV. Unsurprisingly, when he is speaking to me, his SAE is without a trace of this talent. Only once in our sixty minute interview does he use BEV at all, and then he does so very consciously to make a point, when he discusses how he will sometimes "run off a few black lines" to tease his mother, who doesn't tolerate BEV. ("If I really start talking to her like that, then I will . . . risk probably getting, you know, getting ripped to shreds in that . . . house," he explains.) On the other hand, in the beginning of his interview with Max, he speaks BEV, albeit a mild version, comfortably. Thomas has broken his leg, a fact that they refer to in the following conversation:

Max: What about the babes in the choir? (*laughs*)

Thomas: (*laughing*) What about the babes? I love this cat. (*Max laughs*) Man, I love this cat. These babes, I mean, they're kicking. Sherry's hot, man, she's hot, I'm sorry, I just, I was sitting here just (*sighs*), you know. Tried to move up front and stuff (*laughs*).

Max: What'd she do?

Thomas: Huh?

Max: What'd she do?

Thomas: She, she just, what she is, man. (*both laugh*) She just hot, man, that's all there is to it. I need, you know, a lot of attention now cause, you know, I'm all crippled up, you know. The babes just move on over like flies, man.

Max: Uh oh. You're a fly swatter.

Thomas: (*laughs*) Shoot. I don't know what you want to call it, but, you know.

Max: Who you hanging out with now? Who else?

Thomas: Nobody else, man. There is nobody else, man.

Max: Just Sherry.

Thomas: Ain't nothing, man. There ain't eat, there ain't no sleep. (*both laugh*) No, I'm kidding.

Thomas may be using BEV to show that he is not entirely serious—that he is not losing sleep or weight over Sherry but indulging in playful repartee. Although he knows that BEV will signal his playful intent, he announces, "I'm kidding," perhaps in case he is misunderstood.

In his interviews, Thomas expends a great deal of energy on the question of identity, relating it consistently to the use of BEV versus the use of SAE. He provides a good example of a student struggling with the identity problem spawned by negative attitudes toward BEV. He himself holds negative attitudes toward it, and he reports that his mother does. As a result, he strives to speak and write only SAE, and he succeeds well, although there are traces of African-American rhetoric in his written prose. However, he is caught in a bind. While his SAE may please his teachers and his mother, it sometimes alienates him from his African-American peers.

Before beginning college, Thomas evidently believed that if he spoke properly, in SAE, he would be accepted on equal terms by his peers. In his high school, a racially mixed environment, he was comfortable with his identity, he tells me. However, his college experiences showed him two forms of racism, one that holds him at a distance for not using BEV, the other that won't tolerate BEV at all:

Thomas: I felt like, "Well I come from a mixed environment, I've been with this, and I'll be treated the same," and I got here and . . . I hit the real basic attitude that you're black and I'm white. And I didn't know how to handle it the first month I was here. I was just like, well, what do I do now? And then I started going round to the Jester Center, and meeting more black students and getting into more black organizations. Now I feel like well, OK everything's OK. It's fine. But there's always a little something every day that I go home from school and I say, well, I want to be accepted on their side too. I just want to be their friend. I don't want to infiltrate their society. I just want to be a part of the school with them. And I know it will never happen as long as I'm at this school, so.

Valerie: Is this the first time in your life you've come up against a situation like this . . . where you've had to define yourself as black, or, you know?

Thomas: Yeah. Because in high school I was accepted for my merits. Simply. I was . . . an accomplished musician, and I was in an organization, the band, and I was a section leader. And that made me the creme de la creme of all these other musicians and they looked up at me because of my prowess in my field. And that was good enough. I was their friend and I was their mentor. That was good enough. I get here, and the only thing that matters . . . no matter what accomplishments, if I graduate as one of the top UT [University of Texas] students, you know, or best semester student, the best year, year sophomore. It won't matter. What's going to matter is what color my skin is. And . . . I've heard murmurs and things like this when I've been in corridors, like, well, if he does get in it's because the school is stepping down to get him. If he does graduate with honors, maybe he graduated with a 3.0 and not a 3.2. It's just, there's always an undercurrent of, well, we're, you're helping them and because, because they're less than adequate. And it's, I think it's going to be impossible to get around. Cause these students, it's not being woven in by the school, it's being woven in by their parents. And you know, it, how can you fight a generation system like that?

Language is simply another way to discriminate, and Thomas has discovered that all his SAE won't buy him complete acceptance. He has discovered what Bentley calls "attitude interference," which is far more powerful than dialect interference (76).

Spike has an attitude toward BEV similar to, though not as strong as, Thomas's, in that he sees it as something of a joke. Max reminds him: "Now you yourself, from, ah growing up with me, you know, you never really spoke, uh, a lot of slang. And when we'd be kidding around you'd always laugh about it, you know." In his interview with me Spike expresses confusion over how BEV is to be defined, and at first he seems somewhat unwilling to admit that it exists at all. As our conversation illustrates, he has for many years been completely bidialectal, and, since he moved from an all black to a much more mixed high school, his use of BEV has diminished:

Valerie: Do you notice yourself switching [between SAE and BEV] any?
Spike: Um, I guess, I guess that happened pretty much when I was in Middle School. . . . 'Cause I guess I was under a lot of pressure then, I know I was under pressure cause when I played basketball it was definitely all black there . . . and, uh, that wouldn't a went over too well, so I, now that I think back I guess, yeah (*laughs*).

The pressure he refers to is pressure to speak BEV in order to show his solidarity with his group of friends. Notice how he confines his admission of speaking BEV in Middle School to an acceptable domain, the basketball court, where young African-American men typically use a great deal of slang. Unlike Thomas, Spike seems to accept Max's definition of BEV as slang as an acceptable compromise. In semi-formal conversation with Max, who grew up in the same neighborhood as Spike did, he sometimes lapses into a style that uses some BEV forms, primarily BEV slang. Thus he relieves the pressure of conflicting attitudes toward BEV somewhat. He usually speaks and writes in SAE, but he will use BEV, mostly its lexicon, in situations where he feels the need to draw on its covert prestige.

The Advantages: BEV as Blessing

So much for the drawbacks of coming to the academy with a BEV legacy. The advantages, though as substantial, are overlooked, with the result that only the most tenacious BEV speakers can cultivate them and really use them. Divinity has learned quite beautifully some ways in which she can turn her BEV to advantage. In some of her short stories, which she invited me to read and which I found entertaining and artful, she makes extensive creative use of BEV. Once teachers and administrators accept that a knowledge of BEV can carry with it linguistic advantages, many BEV speakers will find themselves not only conforming to the academy but changing it in positive ways. Specifically, the standard language will be open to vitalizing changes from the BEV rhetorical tradition. The trump card held by BEV speakers is the knowledge of a second tradition. They (along with bilingual students) possess a wider repertoire than the average Euro-American student.

By a repertoire is meant the resources available for stylistic exploitation. One principal means by which a speaker or writer creates a stylistic effect is by exploiting language attitudes. While style (that is, a cluster of features that distinguishes a text) shifts quite naturally according to situation, with a change in speakers, setting, or topic, the adroit writer or speaker can manipulate style or, as Blom and Gumperz put it, can create metaphorical style shifts (quoted in Saville-Troike 62–63). Metaphorical style shifting is a conscious manipulation of the expected norms of a situation to create an effect, such as humor, sarcasm, distancing, group identification, or any effect an adept communicator might strive to convey. The metaphorical manipulation of language depends to a large degree on the fact that we assign value to particular linguistic features. Communities share attitudes toward particular registers, manifested by features such as pronunciation, word choice, and syntax. They may likewise share attitudes toward certain tenors of discourse, such as cursing, making promises, or telling stories. The written mode may be valued above the spoken (or vice versa). Or the community may share attitudes toward fields, for example, valuing technical English over non-technical.

Speakers of nonstandard dialects may employ standard dialect features in situations where they wish to show respect or increase their status, assuming, of course, that the standard would be valued in the situation in question. Or speakers of technical jargon (a field of discourse) may employ that jargon at a cocktail party to impress nonspeakers with their intelligence or to demonstrate to the senior members of their field that they deserve notice. Or a writer may employ features of nonstandard or casual spoken discourse to create an impression of informality.[4] As Max and his friends have shown, BEV is often used metaphorically to show group identification. Conversely, SAE can be so used, but, as Thomas discovered, it is sometimes difficult to display such identification simply by virtue of language.

Trudgill tells of an interesting case of whites, British pop singers, attempting to identify with African-Americans by altering their language. The six pronunciation rules that Trudgill finds his pop singers imitate are all "*stereotypically* associated by the British with American pronunciation" [emphasis added] (144). I emphasize *stereotypically* because it is important to acknowledge that in modeling linguistic behavior we often can only approximate the model in idealized terms. If the singers mimic an American accent that conforms to the stereotype their audience holds of American pronunciation, they will have succeeded. The idealized form of the model becomes symbolic.

Trudgill bases his analysis on a theory proposed by Le Page and Tabouret-Keller which states that we model our language and behavior on the language and behavior of the group or role with which we wish to be identified. Their studies of British Caribbean communities in Belize, St. Lucia, and London have focused on exactly this behavior among schoolchildren and have led to a general theory:

> The individual creates for himself the patterns of his linguistic behaviour so as to resemble those of the group or groups with which from time to time he wishes to be identified, or so as to be unlike those from whom he wishes to be distinguished. (181)

The speaker or writer must rely on a stereotype of the group or role with which she wishes to be identified. Her stereotype is to a large extent formed in a community context, and she constructs an ethos to conform to that stereotype. In turn, the audience will interpret her construction in light of their attitudes toward that stereotype. Her success depends, then, on an ability to construct the stereotype as her audience conceives it. This assumption about stereotypes underlies Bartholomae's thesis that students learning to write must "invent" the university by mimicking academic language.

Bartholomae, however, makes us aware of a danger in commanding a wider repertoire. If students' stereotypes of academic language arise from sources significantly different from or divorced from the academic community, they will be more likely to construct faulty stereotypes. If, for example, students attach intellectual value to "big words," as Polo seems to do, they may include "big words" in their stereotype of academic language. The problem is that "big words" without corresponding depth of meaning, "big words" used simply to impress or elaborate, are devalued in many academic discourses—especially English essays.

Still, I wish here to emphasize the positive side of commanding a wider repertoire of styles. To a limited degree, the texts in this study draw on the wider repertoires available to the writers. For example, Divinity used BEV in short stories she showed me, and Shanique used BEV dialogue in her freshman English narrative about a cousin who died. She represented her grandmother's speech as follows: "Shanique, whenever you in trouble or is scared, ask God for help, he'll always help cause that's his job and he's you're friend." And in a dialogue between herself and her grandmother, she wrote:

> "Skim," she called me that because I was so skinny; she said, "Skim, god still loves you, its just that he need Tony right now to help him in Heaven."
> "But what can Tony do, he only fourteen."
> "I know you can't understand right now, but there's reason for everything God does, just keep Tony in your heart and he'll always be with you." . . .
> "But he too big to go in my little chest and he's dead anyhow. How can a big ol' dead boy go in my little chest?"

The dialogue continues in BEV. Of course, in teaching dialogue I had emphasized recreating speech as accurately as possible, and Shanique simply took me at my word, unselfconsciously, I believe. Yet, curiously, when I asked her later to write an essay about a personal experience, she did not use either dialect or dialogue. Perhaps old habits, that proscribe the use of BEV in essay writing, had prevailed.

Another place where I find a consistent use of a written version of BEV is in the letters they wrote for this study. Because of their semi-formal nature and because they are written to peers of the same race, the letters are probably the only clearly acceptable forum for BEV among the types of writing I solicited, at least in these informants' experience. Examples from the letters reveal a limited but obvious attempt to draw on specific features of BEV. There are two probable reasons for this, both having to do with the audience for the letters. Readers include friends (same-sex, same-race peers), the researcher, and the eventual readers of the report on the research, a fact not lost on the letter writers. For the audience of friends, BEV serves metaphorically to establish solidarity. For the other audiences, BEV establishes identity and demonstrates positive prestige. Because the informants are aware that they are participating in a study of "Black English," and because they wish to present themselves and their language in a positive light, they take this opportunity to display their knowledge of "slang." All their uses of BEV are limited to a phrase here or a word there, usually stereotypically associated with BEV.

Laurie, for example, adds a few phrases that merely suggest BEV. The text of her letter follows:

Dear Rene,

What's up, honey? I guess you didn't expect to receive a letter from me, seeing that I practically live down the hall. Well, I was required to write a letter to a friend. So after debating for around fifteen minutes I decided to write you.

I don't know if I've ever told you that I'm glad to have you for a friend. So, since I want to give you a few roses while you're alive, I'll tell you now. [Happy face drawn in margin.]

It's nice to have a friend that I can talk to about "mostly" anything. Ha!! Ha!! You know, honey, somethings you just have to keep to yourself.

I think thus far we have had a wonderful freshman year. Seeing that this year is almost over.

We've had enough laughter to last a life time. From going to parties, Greek Shows, talent shows. I don't know how many nights we've spent talking about guys. Especially, when they piss us off or when they do something extra special for us 2 wonderful, sexy, beautiful girls.

I tell you we simply amaze me. Rene, nothing can compare to our college days at UT. I hope that the friendship we have developed lasts forever. And when you bring your spoiled brat over my house, I'm going whip his * * * behind. [Happy face drawn here.]

LOVE YOU ALWAYS SIS,

Laurie
P. S. FRIENDS FOREVER

Laurie's ending, "And when you bring your spoiled brat over my house, I'm going whip his * * * behind. [Happy face drawn here]," is the most notable approach to BEV. However, in conformity with the polite and conventional tone of the letter, Laurie bowdlerizes the phrase commonly used by BEV speakers, "I'ma whip yo' black ass." She makes sure that propriety is maintained by adding a happy face. She also addresses Rene twice as "honey," in a way reminiscent of African-American females' use of "girl," "child," or "sugar" or other forms of endearment ("What's up, honey?" and "You know, honey, somethings you just have to keep to yourself").

Shanique is more directly draws upon BEV in her letter, the text of which is given below:

La Tonia,

Did you get my letter announcing my engagement to that basketball player I was telling you about? Well, since I hadn't heard from you yet, I'm assuming that cha didn't! Well, I'll bet you're wondering what brought all of this about at such a hurried pace, well, we had an accident, you know, the kind that takes nine months to a lifetime to try and solve, so we figure the best thing to do is get married. The baby isn't due til October so we'll be getting married on June 19th, I do hope you can make it! And one last thing! I really know your mind is about blown so, I'd like to say GOTCHA!! I know it's a little late but APRIL FOOL! [A happy face is drawn in the letter A, and the O's have cross-eyed pupils.] Ha ha, that was a good one huh. Well chil' how're thangs with you and yo man Ron? When are you all planning to come down here? Since I haven't heard from you, (by the way my number is (987) 654-3210) and my address is still the same, I'm assuming that y'all won't make it {to} this weekend for the Texas Relays and the Omega Psi Fie [she writes the Greek letters in the Greek alphabet] stomp down, and the Kappa Alpha Psi's Block Party [again she uses the Greek letters]. What a pity cause I was hoping to entertain you. Well, I'll have fun cause there are going to be plenty of fellows, especially at the Block Party and Omega After Party. Girl it's gonna be sweet! So how are you and Ron, oophs I'm repeating myself! What's the haps at KC? Here there just ain't much except a few girls at the Co-op are kinda getting grumpy & keep bitchin' at each other. And you know me. I just sit back and instigate. Na, just kiddin, I avoid them as much as possible. How's Peg & that guy she was talking to or did she start squeezin' up with ol' Calvin again. By the way I think that weak fella may be running in the relays and if I see him, I'll tell him you said hello and hugs & kisses! I really must go to the meet cause that serious body Richard Taylor is gonna be there and if possible I try and re-acquaint myself. Unless of course, Trent is around, cause that's all I want, Trent. Chil' the other day, I stopped by his room with a friend and girl, I was practically in heaven. My girl left and he and I were alone and we had to talk and get to know each other better then he introduced me to some of the other guys on the basketball team and one guy, Doug Smith, told me I was cute and had a tempting smile cause I have such cute dimples. Girl, you know my head was swollen! Umph! As usual I had to end my happiness by being the good little girl I am and went to class. At least I did get TC to walk me halfway to class cause he had to go to a meeting with his coach.

I know you're going to the Luther Vandross concert so at least be a true friend and buy me a shirt or somethin'. Wished I could go, but you know everyone ain't able to go to {free} concerts for free. (Heffa!) You must give me your number cause sometimes I just want to talk cause writing takes too much effort and I try to exert myself as less as possible! So I've gotta go now cause I'm running outa thangs to chat about. But du hurra & send me your number or give me a buzz so I can tell you about my (suitors) George, James, Wayne, and oh Mark.

Cios!
Diva
Shanique

P.S. Try and come next weekend, its Blackfest '87! Zlive!

Shanique is quite explicitly writing a version of BEV when she includes in her letter the following sentences:
1. Well chil' how're thangs with you and yo man Ron?
2. Girl it's gonna be sweet!
3. What's the haps at KC?
4. Here there ain't much except a few girls at the Co-op are getting grumpy & keep bitchin' at each other.
5. I just sit back and instigate.
6. Chil' the other day, I stopped by his room with a friend and girl, I was practically in heaven.
7. Girl, you know my head was swollen! Umph!
8. Wished I could go, but you know everyone ain't able to go to {free} concerts for free.
9. So I've gotta go now cause I'm running outa thangs to chat about.

Among the stereotypical features of BEV she tries to reproduce in writing are the same terms of endearment Laurie uses (here, "girl" and "chil"), words spelled as pronounced ("chil," "thangs," "yo," "outa"), word choice associated with BEV ("ain't," "haps," "instigate"), and deletion of final consonants ("bitchin'," "chil'"). Most of these features are stereotypically associated with

BEV; for example, the deletion of final letters is common to many speakers, even standard speakers in formal situations, but it is stereotypically associated with nonstandard speech and thus is often seen in "dialect" writing.

On a smaller scale, both Dinese and Divinity, who generally use no BEV in interactions with me or in their more formal writing, use BEV-like forms in their letters. By drawing on BEV-like forms and slang in general, and by selecting "newsy" topics, they create an informal tone quite appropriate to their audience. Dinese's letter sounds generically All-American, yet she seeds it with some terms and expressions that are unmistakably African-American:

> Hey Lisa T.,
>
> What's up with you? I just thought I'd right since I left so fast and we didn't have time to talk.
>
> Right now I'm job-hunting and I'm getting sick of it. The problem is that I'm limited to someplace near the campus. Remember when I told you how bad parking is? Well, I've had one ticket thrown out and I can't afford to let that happen again.
>
> Math is still hard and I got a tutor. But the good news is that my test in anthropology was changed from an 82 to an 89 and it was the highest grade in the class. So even if my prof doesn't curve, and he thinks we don't work hard enough so he may not, I still have a chance to bust "A".
>
> My choir is having College Days and guess who's going to be there: UTA, A&M [a sad face drawn here], Lamar Univ, and Dunbar High School. Yes, girl. Next thing you know we'll be inviting Polytech!
>
> Seriously though, it's going to be great. We also have the Texas Relays going on with people from all over.
>
> [A short paragraph confirming the time of a concert.]
>
> My "love?" life is fine. Charles wants to date again. I might, but I met a seriously nice guy at the Set-Up/Screw/Surprise Your Roommate Party. It was fun, we had to find dates for our roommates!! I've never been to an SYR party—and I've never seen somebody with a hangover like the one girl on our floor had the next day! She was funky drunk. (She wasn't even seen at the place where we went to dance.) [Paragraph continues with a description of the prospective boyfriend. One final paragraph solicits news in a series of questions, and the letter closes.]

Not until paragraph 4, with her use of "Yes, girl" does Dinese use a BEV expression, but when it comes it adds a distinctive African-

American flavor to the banter. The only other such expression is "funky drunk." Divinity's letter is similar. I discuss it in another context in Chapter 3, "Signifying on the Research."

Thomas and Max make the most concerted effort to include BEV in their letters. Thomas's letter is interesting in this respect because elsewhere he makes such a point of being forced to use BEV to conform. His letter seems to draw on BEV as "slang," while it avoids "bad" English. It isn't even formatted like a conventional letter:

> Hey fella! S'up. What's school like? Man, the place is trippin'. Yesterday, I was at the library and, you know how it is, some fabulous babes showed up. Here I was, hair all [illegible] half my outfit dirty, next to this really hot babe. Man, I felt like crawlin under a rock. She was such a babe!! Well, I just decided to get on it and I got to doin' my homework. It was amazing that I finished it with so many ladies fussin' and clamoring and only a couple of tables away. Well, anyways I finished my work and to my surprise, those babes finished too and decided to leave. I tried to walk slow but I still left them behind. (you know [underlined twice] how women lag!) Got into the elevator and headed to 2nd floor, eyes on radar [underlined twice] all the way out of the building. I saw some more of these babes when I got to the power cycle and I dragged my tongue all the way back to the crib. Man, "I need a girlfriend". [Musical notes drawn around the quote.] My crib is damned desolate [underlined twice]. It feels like barren wasteland. No furniture, no people. I need some [illegible word] and some babes. As soon as I get both [underlined twice] I will kick back and scope the glamorous life. Well, Take it slow.
>
> Thomas

Like Shanique, Thomas employs features stereotypically associated with BEV, particularly "trippin'," "man," and a number of words identifiable as slang (e.g., "babes," "kick back," "scope," "crib"). Moreover, he employs many of the strategies found in African-American rhetoric (which I will discuss in more detail in the next chapter), creating a tone of humorous exaggeration that blends boasting about his future success with women and self-deprecation about his present dismal failure as a ladies' man. It must be his desire to be accepted by his peers that prompts him to draw so obviously (yet so subtly) on African-American rhetoric and BEV slang.

Max's letter is equally peppered with "slang":

Dearest Keebler,

I am writing this letter simply to catch up on all the happenings in S.A. [San Antonio]. How's the Babe doing? I'm sure you have her all tide up in knots. Man, I have not heard from you in ages. You know as well as I do that I don't like to write. Since I am gabbing for you, I decided to give you the scoop on all the sceezers on campus. They are all over the yard. My line is still hanging on to me, and the word is out that the Keebler exist. I am going to tell you about yard life since my request for the Dr. Bombay report can't be granted.

My courses are killing me. The computers really aren't kicking. I think that particular class will burst me. I hate that. But you know how it is coming from an all Black high school. We just did not recieve enough info to make it. The Lord willing I shall succeed!!! Another thing is that I'm not really perpetrating. It's just flat out hard. There is no time to chill here. All free time is devoted to you know what. The rest of my time winds up with one of the serious five.

On a good note, God has blessed me with a gift to sing my cares away. Though I realize I can't escape reality, relieving the tension of Long Hornasia helps out alot. We've (the choir), several concerts, and have drawn a large array of crowds. I've gained a little prestige through my vocal chords and have gained alot of rep. A descent rep. at that. Most enjoy coming to see and hear the Innervisions of Blackness [a gospel choir]. I feel the Lord will continue to take us higher and higher.

Time out brother, I just realized that I have had NO decent grub since I left home. The food is totally ospicious on campus. I have gone on several serious diets since my arrival at UT. My perspective is not favorable for homeboys such as ourselves to be subject to this torture. It is beyond me to even describe the dishes prepared for students.

What's happening on the courts? Are you hooping? burning the rock? Slicing and dicing? Netting? Are what? I've not yet ventured back to the courts, but prepare yourself I can still slam on you. In all respect of the word. Lately I have been in the mood to ice it. I've missed the relays, the gym, the babes, the social spectrum of life as a whole. Hopefully I will be on one accord with society again during the short break between summer school. Its illing and no fun and games to be a Black man in a white man's world.

Guess what fella? Kinney came to visit the other day. He had me rolling all afternoon. I even missed physics to trip with him. He said, we all look alike on the yard. Reaboks, box's, shades, loffers, flower shorts, and creepers were our next topic. He said he used to talk about the Q's, nupes, and weys so bad they hated to even come around him. We got into other factors, however dremed back on his UT [University of Texas] days with Will the thrill.

Man, there's so much I could wrap to you about. However, my wrap would not be as affective on these huge cue cards. Therefore, I am going to check you later. I'll probably be in the River Walk City soon and I give you a ring on the telly. Until then chill and keep watch on the main care for me. Everything will and must be copastetic for us. So on the back side and chilly in the most.

P.S. Hold on to the Goodbar!!!

In writing this letter, Max proved himself to be a "good informant" as well as an able user of "slang." Yet overall it is quite standard in grammar and syntax. Thus Max resolves the dilemma of conflicting attitudes toward BEV by limiting it to slang and to particular occasions like letter writing and informal conversation. All these letters employ a survival strategy, one that mirrors racelessness by emphasizing, even celebrating, race. However, the celebration is guarded, for only by equating BEV with slang, that is, with diction, can these academically oriented African-Americans resolve the double-bind of conflicting identity.

What these informants do not seem to realize is that BEV is simply part of a larger system of rhetoric shared by Africans and African-Americans throughout the New World, with deep historical roots. It is a tradition that has survived many upheavals and that has changed considerably over time and geographical distance, yet it endures to be echoed in Thomas's bragging about his success with "babes" or in Max's somewhat ironic lament over being a black man in a white man's world or in Shanique's invocation of the instigator role. It survives in the sense of play and wit displayed in these students' letters and in their talk and their stories.

Notes

[1]Bartholmae's "Inventing the University" makes a convincing argument for this point.

[2]All written essays and letters are reproduced exactly as written by the students.

[3]See also Tucker and Lambert (1969), Seligman, Tucker, and Lambert (1972), Fraser (1973), Williams (1973), and Piché, Rubin, and Turner (1978). Their findings are similar.

[4]Mitchell-Kernan *(Language Behavior,* 74–77) discusses how speakers monitor toward either standard or nonstandard variants, thus signaling social identity.

The African-American Rhetorical Tradition

Before we can understand the writing of the college students involved in this study, we must look to the unique circumstances of their participation in African-American culture. The African-American is likely to have a firmly established rhetoric, one that has roots in Africa and has flourished in its own way in the New World. This rhetoric, described in some detail by Abrahams (especially in "Black Talking"), by Mitchell-Kernan, by Kochman, and by Gates, is acknowledged by its users in their "talk about talk" and in the training of their young. Abrahams provides a fairly comprehensive taxonomy of "talk about talk"; in other words, he charts the speech events most often discussed and acknowledged in those communities he and others have observed. He contends that the existence of special terms for particular speech events, as well as their abundance, argues for their uniqueness ("Black Talking" 241). Speech events are those occasions, such as a wedding reception, that call for particular speech acts, in this case a toast to the bride and groom; or a wedding ceremony, where the vows constitute a speech act. Speech acts are community-defined ways of speaking. Gates, relying on fieldwork by anthropologists, observes that "Black adults teach their children this exceptionally complex system of rhetoric, almost exactly like Richard A. Lanham describes a generic portrait of the teaching of the rhetorical paideia to Western schoolchildren" (75).

Perhaps because scholarly knowledge of this sophisticated tradition is sketchy at best, we often overlook it. Because the primary study of BEV has been by linguists, we assume, quite wrongly, that surface features of grammar, syntax, and phonology define the only differences between BEV and SAE. As I have shown in Chapter 1, attitude interference is more powerful than dialect interference. In this chapter, I will argue that ignorance of African-American rhetoric, not only on the part of Euro-Americans but also on the part of African-Americans, contributes to negative attitudes toward BEV. It causes us to shortchange the verbal skills of African-American students. Not knowing the heritage they draw upon and unable to perceive its artistry, we cannot appreciate their performances. They, in turn, are cheated once again out of their history, a history that would make them proud of their ways of speaking rather than embarrassed by their "bad" English.

Although descriptions of African-American rhetoric differ, mostly because of the difficulties of fixing a dynamic tradition (especially for many researchers, who are outsiders), there is widespread agreement that African-Americans share a heritage of language use that is unique. While individuals may or may not participate actively in this tradition, it is alive and well in many communities, and it has some degree of influence on any African-American aware of or in touch with the vernacular, including the subjects of this study. However, African-Americans sometimes show deep ambivalence toward this tradition, presumably because they know little of its history and because they link it, like BEV, to a lack of status. On the one hand, they associate it with slavery, poverty, ghettos, ignorance. On the other hand, they may find its expressiveness satisfying, especially in the context of church or home or children's games (jump rope rhymes, the dozens, ring play).

Abrahams makes clear the difficulty of accurate description of an African-American rhetoric. For example, its distinction from a general American or Western rhetoric must be made. In this regard, Abrahams does not claim that all speech acts within the BEV community are unique, without analogies among SAE speakers, but that "the range, the intensity, the proliferation of terms, and the importance of such [speech] events are, on the whole, quite different from the configuration of communicative systems found else-

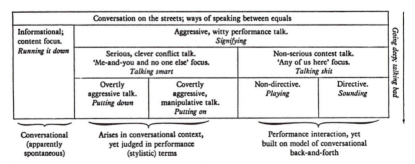

Figure 2–1

where" ("Black Talking" 241). His taxonomy of BEV speech acts is worth reproducing because it provides a recognized introduction to this complex, still not fully understood, system (Figure 2–1).

Abrahams focuses this taxonomy on "street speech" (Baugh's term), which takes place between equals in a street setting, excluding church, school, home, or other institutions associated with respectability. He posits two major categories for street speech: (1) "running it down," which occurs in conversations for informational purposes and (2) "signifying," defined briefly as "aggressive, witty performance talk." According to this model, there are two sorts of signifying, one occurring within dyads (including "talking smart," further divided into "putting down" and "putting on"), and the other occurring in larger groups although on a conversational model (including "talking shit," which divides into "playing" and "sounding") ("Black Talking" 251). Others, for example Mitchell-Kernan, provide slightly different definitions and/or taxonomies from Abrahams'. What is important for our purposes is recognition that BEV speakers may participate in speech events that are unfamiliar to those outside their discourse community. Not only can this be the occasion for miscommunication, it can also be the occasion for missed opportunities. In inter-group communication, outsiders will miss much finesse and artistry.

Community-defined speech acts or speech events are related to community-defined values. Abrahams gives an example of this relationship. African-American communities tend to place values on work and play and on when to speak and when to be silent that differ from those of mainstream Euro-American communities. In the African-American culture, playing accomplished through language is often public, while silence as an attitude of seriousness is a private, home-based matter: "Playing, in fact, is an important way in which one distinguishes oneself in public, and engaging in witty verbal exchanges is one important way of playing" ("Black Talking" 241). Building up a reputation, a "rep," is often accomplished in this public way, through verbal performance and play ("Black Talking" 243-44).

The distinction between the private and the public, the worlds of the home and the street, is a major one when we consider African-American speech events.[1] Although it is in some respects an arbitrary distinction imposed by researchers trying to make sense of a complex system, it is a useful one that is referred to in much of the literature on African-American life. Abrahams has found these dichotomous realms operating widely in African-American folk culture. They are represented in Anglophone Creoles in coastal South America, Central America, the Caribbean, and the Southern United States (*Afro-American Folktales* 10-11). Associated with the street world is masculinity, playing, and "badness," in the sense of aggressive or conflict-oriented behavior and vernacular language. It should be noted that the association of masculinity with street talk (or femininity with proper talk) is as much a folk concept as it is a description of real language use. For example, Mitchell-Kernan observes women engaging in the sorts of talk associated with the street—they are often expert signifiers. Among the subjects I studied, only Shanique, a female, drew to any extent upon smart talk, a form of signifying, or witty repartee. Opposed to the supposedly masculine street is the feminine home, the realm of standard or respectable language (proper or respectable talk) and good behavior. It includes powerful social institutions such as the church and the school. Most of the subjects for this study displayed quite a bit of virtuosity with forms of respectable talk, perhaps because of its association with academics. The males, especially, drew on the respectable forms of fancy talk.

Terminology

Because "proper" has already been extensively used in the literature both positively to mean language that is correct and negatively to mean language that is pretentious, and because I wish to side-step the negative connotations for the present, I will use the term *respectable talk* as a more general term for language that is considered correct and that approaches the standard. To denote language that carries covert prestige and that is nonstandard, I will use the term *bad talk*.

Fancy talk (also sometimes called *sweet talk* in the Caribbean, although sweet talk can also mean respectable talk in a general sense) indicates a style that can be used in either respectable or bad situations. I will attempt a description of fancy talk, with examples, below, but it should be remembered that style—a set of features that typically occur together in particular contexts—is difficult to pin down definitively. Fancy talk generally employs hypercorrect forms and malapropism, Latinate or polysyllabic diction, verbosity, and rhetorical devices such as parallelism or amplification. Although it is typically associated with propriety, it may be found in either the home or the street setting, and can be used "respectably" or in a "bad" way. In the context of propriety, fancy talk is characteristically used by the orators in Caribbean tea meetings, as described below. Although the speech of preachers may be elevated, it is generally not particularly fancy, and they always use some vernacular in their sermons. In the context of the street, fancy talk is often used to impress or dazzle with a display of knowledge, sometimes as a means of romantic persuasion. In both contexts, it is enjoyed for its artistry.

Before I describe fancy talk, I will discuss the wider category of respectable talk.

Respectable Talk

One way of looking at African-American rhetoric is along a dimension of overt/covert prestige. Overt prestige is accorded the language varieties that occur in speech events considered of greatest importance in gaining status in the society at large (work and school, for example, where language moves toward the standard). Covert prestige is accorded language associated with endurance, toughness, and racial identity. Just as there is conflict in African-American attitudes toward BEV, in that it carries connotations of ignorance and high expressiveness at the same time and further conflict in cultural attitudes toward SAE, in that it carries connotations both of education and oppression, there is conflict between the respectable talk of the home and the bad talk of the street.

Any language that approaches the standard and is deemed appropriate for respectable situations is considered correct, or proper. However, the term *proper* can also be used to describe a more stylized and ceremonial register of public oration. Epideictic and homiletic language, used ceremoniously in church sermons and prayers or public oration, would be accorded overt prestige as subsets of respectable talk. In many ways, they are related to other forms of African-American verbal art, including signifying in its various forms and running it down, found in quite a different setting. Sermons are highly influential expressive forms because of their artistry and their prestige. They have probably influenced political oration (Davis 11), and Foster found at least one master teacher who openly avows that sermons provide a model for her lecture style (24).

Respectable talk, which is identified with SAE even though it does not always employ only SAE forms, can carry negative as well as positive connotations. It can be conceived of as snobbish or uppity, especially when it employs hypercorrect forms or is used in inappropriate settings. Scott observes that "overinflected noun forms [e.g., "peoples," "childrens"] are generally considered ungrammatical by black people and are associated with 'talking proper,' which refers to unnecessarily hypercorrect, pretentious uses of language" (338). Other terms for such formal language include "talking fancy," or "intellectual." However, respectable talk is usually accorded overt prestige. It is frequently associated with good manners and may be used to address older women who command respect. It is the language expected of "ladies," and, besides being considered correct, it is decorous and avoids taboo or vulgar expression. On the other hand, insisting on decorum for its own sake, and not to uphold household values, oversteps the boundary and is considered unnecessarily "uppity" (Abrahams, "Negotiating Respect" 64).

Maya Angelou portrays a respectable, though not uppity, lady in *I Know Why the Caged Bird Sings* in the person of Mrs. Bertha Flowers, "the aristocrat of Black Stamps," Arkansas, whom Marguerite Johnson describes as "just as refined as whitefolks in the movies and books" (79). Language marks the difference between Marguerite's illiterate grandmother, Momma, and the educated Mrs. Flowers:

> Why on earth did . . . [Momma] insist on calling her Sister Flowers? Shame made me want to hide my face. Mrs. Flowers deserved better than to be called Sister. Then, Momma left out the verb. Why not ask "How are you, Mrs. Flowers?" With the unbalanced passion of the young I hated her for showing her ignorance to Mrs. Flowers. It didn't occur to me for many years that they were as alike as sisters, separated only by formal education. (78)

But Momma is also a respectable lady, of a different sort, in that she does uphold household values and does avoid talking nonsense or being vulgar. She is merely less educated and less familiar with the standard, less able to express herself in so-called proper English, as Marguerite eventually comes to realize.

A similar mixing of SAE and BEV in a respectable context occurs in the African-American sermon. The reason for this is not always inability to produce correct SAE. It can be a deliberate strategy on the part of the preacher to evoke the covert prestige of BEV and to relate the sacred message of his sermon to the everyday life of his congregation.

In the West Indies, the term for respectable language is *talking sweet* or *sensible*. When used ceremonially, it employs much fancy talk. According to Abrahams:

> This talking sweet is widely observable as the prestige form of serious speech in Afro-American communities throughout the New World. Speaking in this manner elevates the status of the speakers as they address themselves to the important subject of how to endure with dignity and respect. Being able to master such speech is to startle the audience members into attention and provide them with a sense of the possibility of a different kind of mastery—a dominion over their lives and their souls. (*Afro-American Folktales,* 11)

The African roots of sweet talk are suggested by Dillard (who uses the term *fancy talk*): "the use of intentionally glittering and sesquipedalian words and phrases, and . . . disregard for dictionary precision . . . can be documented from many Afro-American sources" (246–47).

Abrahams has observed that the oratorical tradition is so strong in many African-American cultures that formal training in talking sweet is institutionalized. For example, on St. Vincent young men and women are trained by a respected master speaker to perform in the tea meeting, where speakers compete with one another and also with a deliberately difficult audience (Abrahams, "Training of the Man-of-Words"). The speakers excel in talking sweet, which is associated with Standard English, as opposed to broad Creole, and also with behaving well and being sensible ("Training" 17). The speeches at the tea meeting reinforce, as Abrahams puts it, "household values," specifically, rites of passage such as weddings and baptisms that "are strongly associated with the maintenance of the family and household system"

("Training" 18). In the judging of the speakers, value is placed on "mental and verbal agility" ("Training" 27) and on "high" speaking, meaning "not only to ascend the heights of rhetorical inventiveness but to speak long and copiously" ("Training" 25). Handling the audience by keeping their interest and preventing them from heckling are measures of success for both the rhetors and the chairmen, who run the meetings. The most admired rhetors successfully employ elaborate diction to "confuse" (i.e., amaze) the audience and gain "that special kind of active receptiveness characteristic of Afro-American performances" ("Training" 27).

Perhaps the best way to get the flavor of sweet talk is by example, for, as Dillard points out, being often mixed with professional jargon and other types of elaborate discourse or malapropism, it is quite difficult to analyze (254). Abrahams' texts from tea meetings provide excellent examples. The following is from a speech by an advanced student:

> Mr Chairman, judges, ladies and gentlemen, I feel totally ineducate to expiate upon a question so momentously to ourselves. It would be happy and necessary for Africa and the East, for I will be able to express myself before thee. And it is with privilege, hearing my name being called, I stand before you on this rostrum. Chairmen, ladies, and gentlemen, the grandeur of this meeting fills my mind with job and remitting felicity and, like Alexander the Great when he having manifest his vicinity at Alexandria and thus explain in the language Athenian, *careto claret primus disjecta membera* of the festivity. ("Training" 24)

Abrahams reports on numerous occasions in the West Indies where sweet talk is practiced, including versions of tea meetings on a number of islands.

In Tobago, for instance, he reports the use of sweet talk at wakes (bongos), at *thanksgiving ceremonies* (where thanks is publicly given for any good fortune such as recovery from illness), at storytelling sessions, at sermons, and at Carnival performances, especially the mas', performed by masqueraders. The speeches of the mas' are typically "heroic in tone and diction," and "they always rhyme, use inflated rhetoric, and strongly hyperbolic diction" (*Man-of-Words* 4-5). Here is an example:

> I call my King and Commander not to keep that in the memorandum. Let us bring them under perpendicular rules and regulation.

> When they call for food let us give them bread and saffron.
> When they call for water, let us give them Candice Lotion.
> (*Man-of-Words* 6)

Numerous examples are given in *The Man-of-Words in the West Indies*, and each is wonderful in its flash and display. One example shows a female, this time from Nevis, as a sweet talker. Following is an excerpt from her wedding toast:

> As I stand on this happy occasion giving my best wishes to all Mr. Bride and Mrs. Bride—when I look around at this domicile it makes me feel *Homa Doma*, which is to say it makes me feel like a new girl. Mr. and Mrs. Bride, this feast reminds me of the feast of Belshazzar. . . . Mr. and Mrs. Bride, I will not take up any more of your precious and your valuable time. Ima dance *pasear de boca* come and take—a kiss from the lips all time touch the heart.
>
> To the Ladies and Gentlemen, inside and outside. Please listen to my melodious anthem, which is to say, my beautiful voice, to Mr. Bride sir. (*Man-of-Words* 36)

Sweet talk in the Caribbean uses to its extreme form the style Dillard calls fancy talk. He gives two basic characteristics of fancy talk, both displayed in these examples: first, "flashy vocabulary, often beyond appropriateness to the subject under discussion from the point of view of the speaker of Standard English" and second, "'poetic' diction, or 'highly seasoned' talk" (249). The judgment of the audience concerning such things as appropriateness depends upon their knowledge not of SAE *per se* but of the culture that values fancy talk. In other words, the audience that knows nothing of the tea meeting, the mas', or the wedding toast and that gets no pleasure from the poetic sound of the language will certainly hear the example just quoted very differently from what the speaker intended. And the speaker may be judged by such an ignorant audience as being herself ignorant or comical, of "misusing" or "murdering" the "King's English."

Fancy talk can occur both in speaking and in writing. It generally calls attention to itself as a performance style by employing some or all of the features listed below:

1. Ornate, polysyllabic diction, often associated with the grand style that Cicero and Quintilian found appropriate to oratory, especially epideictic oratory;
2. Neologisms, often invented on the spot;
3. Foreign words or phrases, especially Latin; sometimes the

       foreign words are invented, that is, they are merely for-
       eign-sounding;
4. Malapropism;
5. Ornate rhetorical figures, especially amplification, copi-
    ousness, parallelism, and alliteration;
6. Circumlocution, or verbosity, often related to the intent to
    amplify as a rhetorical strategy;
7. Unusual syntax, such as inversions, omissions, and
    changes in the normal patterns of English syntax; and
8. Attention to sound in at least equal proportion as atten-
    tion to sense.

Impressionistically, fancy talk is easy enough to recognize, in that
it is a fairly obvious bid on the part of the speaker or writer to
sound "fancy," that is, educated and erudite. Furthermore, the
speaker is generally performing and is expected to dazzle and
move the audience with verbal agility.

    Ingraham and Lynch observe forms of fancy talk. Ingraham's
accounts, overtly racist and probably distorted, are valuable in
that they call attention to the phenomenon and give an example of
attitudes toward it. He reports in 1835 of questioning a Southern
slave:

> "Ben, how did you like the sermon today?" I once inquired of one
> who, for pompous language and high-sounding epithets, was the
> Johnson of negros—"Mighty obligated wid it, master, de 'clusive
> 'flections werry destructive to de ignorum." (248)

Lynch's descriptions of tea meetings on Barbados are particularly
vivid, for example:

> And so the speaker would lead his impressed and admiring hearers,
> the heads of the ladies nodding approval, the mouths of small boys
> hanging open with wonderment, through the labyrinthine maze of
> classical eloquence, always ending with "And now, Ladies and
> gents, I will redound to my sanctum sanctorum." (243)

    Dillard, like Abrahams, explains that there is some associa-
tion of fancy talk with Standard English (251). But this association is not absolute. Another way to understand the connection
between Standard English and fancy talk is to consider how fancy
talkers regard the standard. We cannot assume that they regard it
in the same light as the majority in the dominant culture. In fact,
as fancy talkers demonstrate, they have alternate ways of using

Standard English, ways the dominant culture does not appreciate or understand: "fancy talkers," Dillard explains, "have never been bound by schoolmarmish injunctions to use the plain word where it will do, to avoid words with which one is not entirely familiar, etc." (247). Thus, although fancy talk is indeed associated with propriety and "proper" English, it also has a subversive dimension in relation to the standard language of the dominant culture.

African-American sermons and prayers offer a case in point. On the one hand, they do employ a modest fancy talk. Rosenberg actually says the language of sermons he recorded was not fancy. He noted few periodic sentences or polysyllabic and Latinate words. His explanation is that such words would interfere with meter and with communicating with the congregation (101–102). Certainly the preponderance of the simple diction of the King James Bible is influential in this respect. But Pipes (134–35) and Jones-Jackson (24) have found some fancy talk in sermons and prayers, used quite clearly for effect, often for the way they contributed to making the discourse sonorous.

On the other hand, sermons and prayers employ in equal measure the vernacular, in an attempt again to tap its covert prestige and to bring a religious message to a secular level, where it can be more meaningful for the ordinary person. Davis, limiting himself to sermons, discusses what he calls this "bipolar tension" between "concretely secular" and "abstractly churchly or sacred perspectives" as evidenced in the sermon text by theme (104–105; also, Pitts); the best sermons, those most appreciated as art, achieve a careful balance between these poles. The performance he rates most highly not only achieves this balance but also uses a great many BEV forms, although Davis notes only the secular themes. Pitts observed inflation of BEV forms, especially during the climax of sermons, by younger preachers, those without established congregations, which he attributes to their wish to "increase their value and esteem before a crowd" (219).

The status of the sermon as a high form of African-American verbal art is undisputed. Davis has studied the structure of the sermon, which is uniform throughout the United States. It is patterned symmetrically and rhythmically around a theme stated in the exordium (usually a Bible verse) and developed in smaller units that cohere to it by use of "thematic bridges." This sacred theme must be explicated and discussed in the light of secular experience (Davis 60–61). The sermon's structured argument is characterized by an array of rhetorical devices, including allusions to and direct quote from Scripture, metaphor and simile, alliteration, repetition (such as anaphora and epistrophe), parallel structure. Also essential are paralinguistic features such as complicated feet and hand movement, heavy breathing during the climax, and the chanted quality of the performance. Because the performance is affective, it elicits the active participation of the congregation in responses that show understanding of the message and appreciation for the art. When such responses are not forthcoming, the preacher knows the performance did not go well.

According to Jones-Jackson, the oral prayer tradition of the Gullah-speaking Sea Islands is equally rhetorically sophisticated. She likens the prayers' style to the grand style of Ciceronian and Quintilianesque tradition, "alive with prolific imagery, maxims, puns, understatements, and cultural references to which the audience understands, relates, and responds with enthusiasm and zeal" (23). Like the sermon, the prayer is always structured, beginning with an introduction that provides a salutation, an appeal, and a peroration, often a quotation. Prayers are delivered by laypersons as well as clergy, quite frequently without preparation, and some congregation members are considered adept at this sort of performance. Jones-Jackson notes prayers lasting from one to twenty-five minutes (25).

An excerpt from a sermon by Bishop E. E. Cleveland, recorded by Davis and rated highly for its artistry, gives at least the flavor of this complicated art form. After quoting from Isaiah 59 ("[Y]our sins have hid His face from you/That He cannot hear"), Cleveland announces his theme:

> The fault
> Is not in the Lord
> You are just not ready
> God said here in Isaiah, the fifty-ninth chapter
> The fault ain't in Me
> I know you're about to turn atheist
> You're about to say there ain't no God
> You're just about to say I'm dead
> But the fault ain't in Me
> You're just not ready
> For My blessings
> Hallelujah to God

> Your iniquity have separated between you and your God
> And your sins have hid His Face from you
> You speak lies and perverse things
> Thank God
> And it's because of you that you can't get the blessing
> It doesn't mean that you can't get married now
> Plenty folks get married
> You haven't got your blood test
> You haven't got your license
> You haven't got your divorce
> It's not final
> You got six more months to go
> So you are not ready
> To get married
> And folks are getting married every day
> Glory to God. (Davis, 115–16)[2]

In this example we see both a theme ("You're just not ready to accept salvation") and the development of the first supporting argument ("Just like you give excuses for not being ready to marry and live instead in sin"). We also see both secular and sacred language, parallel structure, and allusions as well as direct reference to Isaiah 59.

Heath has observed that the performance of sermons, prayers, and hymns is extended into many other spheres of life in Trackton, the African-American community she studied for ten years:

> [T]here is an oral performance pattern of building a text which uses themes and repetitions with variations on these themes. The young children follow this pattern in practicing and playing in their language learning; older siblings use it when they entertain the community with their songs and games; it permeates greetings, and leavings, and parts of stories. Often a formulaic phrase expresses an essential idea, but this phrase is for building from, and as such is continually subject to change as individuals perform and create simultaneously. (*Ways with Words* 211)

Her observation—that language used in one context influences language used in another context—is important to my thesis that African-American rhetoric must have an influence on the way African-American students construct academic discourse. I will discuss this at greater length in the chapters that follow. There are other aspects to African-American rhetoric to explore first, those that arise from another side of community life.

Talking Bad

Marguerite's shame at Momma in *I Know Why the Caged Bird Sings* comes from her association of Momma's speech with "talking bad" (or, as Abrahams reports, *talking country, broad, patois,* or *broken*). Talking bad is primarily associated with the street corner, the good-time world of males, and nonstandard or rural dialects or creoles. It is a way of speaking apart from the dominant culture as well as from school and church. Just as respectable talk moves toward the standard, bad talk moves toward the nonstandard. For many BEV speakers, bad talk has its share of positive connotations; in Labov's terms, it carries covert prestige because it is associated with folk and ethnic values. It may also, as for Marguerite, carry negative associations, especially for those who aspire to upward social mobility and who see their membership in the vernacular culture as a handicap. For example, in St. Vincent talking bad is also called *talking nonsense* or *playing the fool* and is associated with rudeness ("Training of the Man-of-Words" 17).

Just as talking respectable serves a function at the tea meetings of St. Vincent, talking bad serves a function in the culture, primarily as the language of subversion. While talking respectable reinforces household values, talking bad undermines and challenges them: "There are certain ceremonial occasions (like Carnivals and wakes), in which it is regarded as appropriate and encouraged" ("Training" 17). Not only does talking bad undermine household values; it celebrates the counter values of licentious performances ("Training" 18). For example, it is usually, in its most broad version ("talking black"), the language of folktales:

> [Folktales] represent a kind of linguistic liberation that contrasts both with the way Old Master talked and with the ornamental speech-making that takes place in church or at wedding feasts, baptisms, and other formal occasions. In this situation, talking black is the language of action and energy and is strongly associated with males and public places (the street corner, the rum shop, the crossroads, wherever *hanging out* . . . takes place). (*Afro-American Folktales* 10-11)

Another example comes from the tea meetings, where designated members of the audience, *pit boys*, try to confuse the orators with rudeness ("Training" 20).

As I mentioned in the previous section, the African-American sermon, although it lies in the domain of respectability, employs "bad" talk as a matter of course. Likewise, at least one teacher has been shown to use bad talk in the traditionally respectable domain of a community college class. Just as a brief example, Mrs. Morris, in a management class, weaves BEV into her lecture: "you better learn that accounting to make sure nobody don't cheat you out of your money or mess with your books" (Foster 12).

As the pit boys demonstrate, the wit and intelligence displayed by talking respectable can also be displayed by talking bad. In the context of the street, talking bad as a verbal art is not simply the use of nonstandard dialect but of those rhetorical strategies associated with the speech events named in Abraham's taxonomy (see Figure 2–1). Such talk is often aggressive or flamboyant. Talking bad makes use of insult, boasting, bragging, mimicry (called *marking*), and every conceivable form of humorous exaggeration.[3] In some cases, as in sounding or the dozens (ritual insult games) or the recitation of toasts or folktales, the rhetoric is highly structured and traditional, while in other cases, as in running it down or talking smart, it is spontaneous and quite individualized, often taking the form of repartee. Kochman has discussed the importance of high style (an individualized flair) and force ("animation and vitality") as attributes of African-American verbal art (*Black and White Styles* 107; 130).

As we saw in Chapter 1, Thomas' letter makes use of some of the strategies used by bad talkers, although he has purged it of any nonstandard grammar:

> Hey fella! S'up. What's school like? Man, the place is trippin'. Yesterday, I was at the library and, you know how it is, some fabulous babes showed up. Here I was, hair all [illegible] half my outfit dirty, next to this really hot babe. Man, I felt like crawlin under a rock. She was such a babe!! Well, I just decided to get on it and I got to doin' my homework. It was amazing that I finished it with so many ladies fussin' and clamoring and only a couple of tables away. Well, anyways I finished my work and to my surprise, those babes finished too and decided to leave. I tried to walk slow but I still left them behind. (you *know* [underlined twice] how women lag!) Got into the elevator and headed to 2nd floor, eyes on *radar* [underlined twice] all the way out of the building. I saw some more of these babes when I got to the power cycle and I dragged my tongue all the way back to the crib. Man, "I need a girlfriend". [Musical notes drawn around the quote.] My crib is damned *desolate* [underlined twice]. It feels like

barren wasteland. No furniture, no people. I need some [illegible word] and some babes. As soon as I get *both* [underlined twice] I will kick back and scope the *glamorous life*. Well, Take it slow.

Thomas

Thomas employs self-deprecation in a humorous and slightly exaggerated way, portraying himself as a hang-dog scholar who follows the ladies with no success (he has to blame them for being too slow!). Particularly vivid are his images of "crawlin under a rock," following girls with his "eyes on radar," dragging his tongue all the way home. His "crib" (apartment) he describes melodramatically as a "barren wasteland." He almost boasts about how lonely and desolate he is. He insults the women who attract his attention by calling them "babes" and portraying them as "fussin' and clamoring" and lagging. In spite of his self-deprecation, nothing in this letter invokes genuine sympathy, however, and surely it is not intended to do so. On the contrary, he ends with a mild brag that he will eventually lead the glamorous life— as soon as he gets it together, which is surely only a matter of time. In short, Thomas puts on a bad talker performance to amuse his friend with his adventures in college.

In some speech events associated with the street, particularly *running it down* or some types of *putting on*, the style used will be fancy—with a preponderance of hypercorrect forms, polysyllabic and Latinate words, verbosity, malapropism, and so on. The folktales reveal fancy talkers as stereotyped characters. Generally, they are figures of ridicule and fun that represent what members of the culture should avoid (Dance). There is the preacher, whose legendary hypocrisy is the butt of endless jokes; he uses his glibness for material gain and female favors. Dance mentions the connection between the folkloric character of the preacher and "big words": "The Minister has been the butt of jokes from the time of slavery until the present, not only as an egotistical, vain leader, but also as an ignorant lover of big words" (41).[4] Then there is the *cat* or the *bad nigger* who, unlike his hypocritical counterpart, has no pretensions of being good but revels in his badness. He signifies, meaning he uses the language of indirection to get what he wants, perhaps to talk himself out of trouble (*cop a plea*) or to court women. Both the preacher and the cat use words to dazzle, to confuse, to impress (like the pit boys), all for the purpose of gaining power. They are the rhetors of Plato's nightmares, using their skill with language as a tool to manipulate. Their ability to talk bad works to their advantage, helping them construct an ethos of intelligence, wit, and control. While it is common knowledge that they can be disruptive or dangerous, their artistry as performers is highly valued. As a form of *putting on*, or establishing dominance, fancy talk can be applied to romantic persuasion, in which case it is also called *sweet talk*. This is the common use of the term, familiar even to those outside the community.

Fancy talk can be employed in *running it down*, that is, in providing information. This was observed by Hannerz in an ethnographic study of a ghetto street in Washington, D. C. in the late sixties; the so-called "streetcorner mythmakers," the black males who spent leisure hours on the street, employed fancy talk to enhance their reputation. Hannerz mentions a character type noted by others, including Abrahams, who is recognized by his peers as an *intellectual*, someone who shows by his talk that he is knowledgeable about some subject. For example, there is Bee Jay. Hannerz describes him as follows:

> Middle-aged, usually unemployed, and in poor health from too heavy drinking, [he] speaks of the years he claims to have spent at an Ivy League college, casually drops in garbled quotes from Socrates, Oscar Wilde and assorted other notables, and repeatedly returns to the topic of his hunting trip to Africa as Ernest Hemingway's valet. This, plus an astounding vocabulary, certainly make many of his friends and neighbors recognize him as an intellectual. . . . Yet just about everybody has strong doubts about the truth of some of his stories. (106)

Hannerz, as an ethnographer, attends to details about Bee Jay that are not of great concern to this discussion, i.e., his poverty and poor health, but what is of interest is Bee Jay's use of language to construct an ethos that will bring him some measure of respect on the street. Everybody recognizes a certain amount of exaggeration in Bee Jay's talk, but his manner of speaking also earns him status as an intellectual. Interestingly, the male subjects in the present study use the term *intellectual* in a way reminiscent of Hannerz's Washington, D. C. informants, as I describe in Chapter 4.

Abrahams ("Black Talking" 252) mentions *rifting*, another form of running it down, as employing fancy talk, although what Labov, et al. describe as rifting is rather different, more formal and ritualized than what Abrahams describes. Labov and his fellow researchers find that rifting is particularly devoted to relating occult knowledge, Black Muslim ideology in the cases they investigated. They describe

> an elevated high flown delivery which incorporates a great many learned Latinate words, spelling out the uncontracted function words with characteristic level and sustained intonational pattern that lays extra stress and length on the last stressed word. The occult knowledge which is delivered in this way is "heavy knowledge," "heavy stuff," or "heavy shit"; and too heavy for outsiders to understand. (Vol II, 136)

Rifting employs fancy talk in two respects: (1) "the function . . . is to impress others with the depth of one's knowledge, and it is quite plausible that complex syntax would play a role in this effort"; and (2) "rifting draws heavily on the traditional preaching style of the Southern Baptists, evangelical religions, and the store-front churches of Harlem" (Vol. II, 137).

Attitudes Toward Fancy Talk

Fancy talking styles in both the respectable and the bad versions have been parodied and lampooned by Euro-Americans and African-Americans alike, although Euro-Americans certainly have been harsher and more frequent in their attacks. Dillard (*Man-of-Words*) and Abrahams (*Afro-American Folktales*) report on a number of historical accounts of slave gatherings where African-Americans are portrayed by ignorant whites as imitating their masters' eloquence or aspiring to their facility with English. The minstrel show provides the most familiar example:

> On those occasions when the cool, high style of self-presentation was observed, however—blacks displaying themselves to one another in what today might be called "styling out"—the white reaction was commonly one of amused derision, seeing the effort as simply one more bungled black attempt to imitate white cultural practices. Styling-out was expressed in a wide range of dress and a parading style of public walking . . . as well as in oratorical forms of speech. These oratorical forms were mimicked in hypercorrect and ultracor-rupted fashion in the "fancy talk" speeches, also found in black-face shows, providing white anecdotalists with a subject for many of their most popular routines, stories in which a character attempts to use

jaw-breaking words but manages only to come up with mala-propisms. (*Afro-American Folktales* 12)

Such ridicule of a culture's rhetoric often has remarkable endurance. Others, including Stephen Crane in "The Monster," Ingraham, and Lynch evince the attitude that African-American fancy talk results from a simple mimicry of whites.

Crane's character Henry Johnson is a dandified chauffeur. The very description of Henry echoes grandiloquent use of paral-lelism: "it was plain from Henry's talk that he was a very hand-some negro, and he was known to be a light, a weight, and an eminence in the suburb of the town, where lived the larger num-ber of the negroes" (451). Crane's bemused attitude toward Henry's "airs" becomes apparent in the scene in which Henry courts Bella Farragut. Wearing his lavender trousers and straw hat "with its bright silk band," he makes a stately appearance at the Farragut home, where he is received by Mrs. Farragut: "The fat old woman met him with a great ivory smile, sweeping back with the door, and bowing low. 'Walk in, Misteh Johnson, walk in. How is you dis ebenin', Misteh Johnson—how is you?'" (456). The scene ends with a blatant comparison between the participants and mimicking apes, both in manners and in speech:

> After a great deal of kowtow, they were planted in two chairs oppo-site each other in the living-room. Here they exchanged the most tremendous civilities, until Miss Bella swept into the room, when there was more kowtow on all sides, and a smiling show of teeth that was like an illumination.
>
> The cooking-stove was of course in this drawing room, and on the fire was some kind of a long-winded stew. Mrs. Farragut was obliged to arise and attend to it from time to time. Also young Sim came in and went to bed on his pallet in the corner. But to all these domes-ticities the three maintained an absolute dumbness. They bowed and smiled and ignored and imitated until a late hour, and if they had been the occupants of the most gorgeous salon in the world, they could not have been more like three monkeys.
>
> After Henry had gone, Bella, who encouraged herself in the appro-priation of phrases, said, "Oh, ma, isn't he divine?" (456–57)

Irony underscores Crane's apparent belief that refinement is out-side the African-American experience and that any sign of cul-ture, manner, or eloquent speech must be accounted for by slavish imitation.

Ingraham's book, *The Southwest by a Yankee* (original publication, 1835) provides another example. It is racist and ethnocentric. Describing "Negro Magniloquence," itself a rather grandiose term, he writes:

> The males prefer collecting in little knots in the streets, where, imitating the manners, bearing, and language of their masters, they converse with grave faces and in pompous language, selecting hard, high-sounding words, which are almost universally misapplied, and distorted, from their original sound as well as sense to a most ridiculous degree—astounding their gaping auditors 'ob de field nigger class,' who cannot boast such enviable accomplishments. (56)

African-American poet James Weldon Johnson, author of *God's Trombones*, a volume of poems inspired by folk preaching, has something to say about this stereotyping:

> Gross exaggeration of the use of big words by these preachers, in fact by Negroes in general, has been commonly made; the laugh being at the exhibition of ignorance involved. What is the basis of this fondness for big words? Is the predilection due, as is supposed, to ignorance desiring to parade itself as knowledge? Not at all. The old-time Negro preacher loved the sonorous, mouth-filling, ear-filling phrase because it gratified a highly developed sense of sound and rhythm in himself and his hearers. (9)

There is no doubt that the African-American style of fancy talk has deep roots in both African and New World traditions and that it relies not only on the dictionary definitions of words but also on their sounds and their connotations.

When ridicule of this tradition comes from a dominant class, those whose language is under fire will find themselves in conflict: by following their own rhetorical strategies, they run the risk of constructing an ethos that is read by their oppressors according to negative stereotypes. In reaction, they often sharply separate their uses of language according to audience. To err by using BEV dialect or rhetoric with the wrong audience could cause them to lose face. Their dilemma is eased by the fact that BEV and SAE are limited to very different domains, but, especially for those who have limited contact with SAE or less ability as bidialectals, the problem can intensify in situations where language is not rigidly prescribed. A good example is provided by Shanique, who speaks to me using many BEV features (although she writes only in SAE). One explanation for this is that our conversations take place outside the classroom, where she plays the role of my assistant; language conventions are not rigidly prescribed in this situation, though they tend toward the informal, and she feels comfortable and natural with me. If, however, I were prejudiced against BEV, or even against the use of BEV in semiformal situations, Shanique would have made a grave error.

Disdain for fancy talk can come from the vernacular as well as the dominant culture. For example, Scott, quoted earlier, claims that "overinflected noun forms [eg., "peoples," "childrens"] are generally considered ungrammatical by black people and are associated with 'talking proper,' which refers to unnecessarily hypercorrect, pretentious uses of language" (338). Mitchell-Kernan makes a similar claim: "Needless and extreme circumlocution is considered poor art" ("Signifying" 173). Such statements cannot be taken at face value, for they judge uses of language outside any context, and rhetorical uses of language are highly sensitive to appropriateness as determined by context. There are times when fancy talk is perceived as "uppity" or "saddity," that is, as pretentious, and there are times, for example at tea meetings, when it is valued for its artistry. In the latter case, the more circumlocution, the better.

There is a similarity in the African-American appreciation of fancy talk and the claim by both Cicero and Quintilian that the grand style is the most sublime, requiring the most skill and having the greatest impact upon an audience. The grand style, after all, shares many features with fancy talk—the rhetorical flourishes and use of figurative language, the use of grandiose diction, the association with performance and artistry. In the popular imagination, at least, there is an enduring respect for grandiloquent language and the erudition it conveys.

Needless to say, there is a corresponding mistrust, perhaps because grandiloquent language is associated with persuasion and persuasion with manipulation. The Aristotelian prejudice in style leans toward moderation, neither highly figured and grand nor overly plain. According to this view, style should not call attention to itself but be natural and appropriate. To those unfamiliar with fancy talk as an acknowledged style, then, it would seem highly extravagant and unnatural, neither dignified nor appropriate. By the same token, those who maintain the "style is the man," or that it expresses character, would find fancy talk insincere, bombastic, pompous—not in the context of its use, but because of its very exuberance and circumlocution, its malapropism and its improvisational character.

Verbal Art

Fancy talk, then, is one way a good talker can establish a reputation as a wit or intellectual, and he or she may use this reputation to get respect or romance, to assert or maintain dominance, or for any number of manipulative reasons. African-Americans generally place a strong emphasis on verbal art, and fancy talk is simply one style employed. The whole range of street speech acts classified by Abrahams are considered art forms, as are the telling of folktales, the quoting of proverbs, sermonizing, orating, and lecturing. In short, African-Americans constantly evaluate speech for its artistry, as their talk about talk attests.

The artistry of the ways of speaking at home and on the street is recognized, commented upon, and appreciated by speakers of the vernacular. Comment upon failed performances makes it clear that aesthetic standards are applied. For example, John Edgar Wideman describes how a poor performance detracts from ethos. His brother, Robby, in prison for murder, tells about a "lame," meaning a poor performer, a white man who is being set up for a con who "thinks he's cool but . . . messes up":

> [H]e was one suspicious dude. Never take his eye off you. And talking trash, too. Street talk. Like some them young white guys. But this dude a bald-head, potbelly chump. Talking that lame. Hey, man this and Hey, man that shit. Laying down his feeble rap like he goes for bad and do. (144)

The lame's language, his "feeble rap" gives him away. He is trying to project cool without carrying it off, thus earning contempt from Robby. To perform well verbally is no easy feat. The audience is demanding and protective practices such as Goffman describes—tact, for example—are not readily extended.

According to Dillard, attempts like that reported by Wideman's brother to imitate BEV styles like fancy talk validate them as neither idiosyncratic or personal talent but as institutions. Some segments of Anglo culture, typically the more marginalized or rebellious, identify with black culture, expressing it through language: "The proof of the pudding . . . seems to be in the imitation; those who seek to achieve the same effects apart from the tradition achieve only a watered-down usage of ethnic slang" (252). Ethnic slang, of course, is only a small part of the tradition. But the substitution of part of the tradition for the whole represents the partial competence of those outside the culture. The less involved the imitator is in the culture with which she wishes to be identified, the farther her stereotyped version of its members' language may be from its actual form. A sprinkling of African-American slang, sometimes used incongruously, may serve as a sign that a speaker wishes to be identified with African-American culture (Trudgill; Le Page and Tabouret-Keller).

We have seen that Max, Spike, Thomas, Polo, and Dinese identify BEV as "slang(s)." Their doing so does not result from partial competence but from the need to reconcile conflicting attitudes toward BEV and African-American rhetoric. While there is covert prestige attached to BEV by most African-American speakers (see, for example, Mays' study of school children's attitudes), negative associations are also strong.

I have limited my focus in this chapter to a small number of styles used in African-American rhetoric. I do so because they are the styles I can identify as being somehow influential in the writing of the subjects of this study. Max, Polo, and Thomas show strong signs of being influenced by the fancy talking tradition and by the homiletic tradition. Shanique and Divinity draw on the covert prestige of bad talk, especially on witty smart talk, though in very different ways. For Shanique the use of bad talk is unselfconscious and natural, for Divinity it is a way to enhance her narrative style in her creative compositions. Shanique is also adept at storytelling, and she uses many conventions of the African-American folktale. Dinese and Laurie are influenced by their attitudes toward respectable talk. They make an obvious attempt to sound respectably ladylike. Dinese pulls this off more successfully than Laurie because she does not betray herself with nonstandard forms. Spike and Thomas have similar concerns with respectability. Thus, the subjects of this study are influenced by a rhetoric that is unfamiliar to many of their teachers and peers in a school setting. As I will show in the chapters that follow, it is a rhetoric that employs styles often at odds with the prejudices and idiosyncrasies of academics. Yet it is equally a rhetoric with great expressiveness that can strengthen academic discourse.

Notes

[1] A full discussion of these traditions is found in Abrahams' *The Man-of-Words in the West Indies*. See, for example, p. 3.

[2] The line breaks indicate rhythmical units.

[3] Kochman makes a distinction between this sort of bragging ("a serious form of self-aggrandizement") and boasting ("obvious exaggeration" in which "no correlation between words and deeds need exist"). While boasters are not held accountable for their claims, braggarts are. Moreover, while it is socially acceptable to brag about one's talents and abilities, it is unacceptable to go on about personal possessions or social status (*Black and White Styles* 63–66).

[4] Dance notes that the preacher also provides a positive role model, especially for youth. She cites an interview with John M. Ellison, retired president of Virginia Union University, who told her, "when I grew up, the first person I knew of a professional nature was my minister." She adds that this is a typical statement which her own experience as an African-American supports (42).

Signifying on the Research

A s I explained in Chapter 2, signifying is one of the major speech acts to be found in African-American rhetoric. It is what Abrahams has called "aggressive, witty performance talk" ("Black Talking" 251). Mitchell-Kernan points out its primary function is to comment critically but indirectly upon another's behavior or upon some situation: "an alternative message form, selected for its artistic merit" ("Signifying" 165). Gates goes so far as to call signifying the "trope of tropes" of African-American rhetoric because he finds it primary to the African-American aesthetic, insofar as comments upon another's performance (past masters, so to speak) evolves into new performances. Individual style is played out by working with and against community traditions.

The classic example of signifying was collected by Mitchell-Kernan ("Signifying" 166–67). Although it is frequently quoted, I include it for the reader's convenience and for its illustrative excellence. Signifying just cannot be appreciated in the abstract. In this excerpt, Barbara, Mary, and Mitchell-Kernan (R for Researcher) are in Barbara's home, and Mitchell-Kernan is on her way out:

BARBARA: What are you going to do Saturday? Will you be over here?
R: I don't know.
BARBARA: Well, if you're not going to be doing anything, come by. I'm going to cook some chit'lins. [Rather jokingly] Or are you one of those negroes who don't eat chit'lins?
MARY: [Interjecting indignantly] That's all I hear lately—soul food, soul food. If you say you don't eat it, you get accused of being saditty [affected, considering oneself superior]. [Matter of factly] Well, I ate enough black-eyed peas and neck-bones during the depression that I can't get too excited over it. I eat prime rib and T-bone because I like to, not because I'm trying to be white. [Sincerely] Negroes are constantly trying to find some way to discriminate against each other. If they could once get it in their heads that we are all in this together maybe we could get somewhere in this battle against the man. [Mary leaves.]

BARBARA: Well, I wasn't signifying at her, but like I always say, if the shoe fits, wear it.

Mitchell-Kernan presents further evidence to demonstrate quite clearly that Barbara was indeed signifying at Mary.

At face value, there is nothing peculiarly African-American about signifying. It is the high level of African-American sensitivity to this way of speaking that merits its inclusion as a cultural practice. It is a named speech act, as Barbara demonstrates by using the term, and African-Americans, although they may not always call it signifying, are aware it can be used effectively (or be effectively used against them).

I was fascinated to discover that the eight informants in my study were signifying on the research (and often on me as the researcher, though tactfully). I say I *discovered* this because I was usually unable to perceive it when it occurred; it was far too polite and indirect, and I was not prepared, as a white researcher, for this strategy. In fact, I was quite taken aback the first time I read Divinity's narrative essay, which is a study in signifying. I had found the prompt successful in eliciting narratives and had used it in many classes: "Write about a time you broke a rule or broke the law." Divinity used this prompt as the focal point for a virtual tirade of signifying but in written, essay form. Her essay, reproduced below, targets me in no uncertain terms:

According to some sociology test, I'm supposed to be pretty deviant. Some Klansman somewhere would say I'm deviant because I am black. Even some whites less bigoted than a Klansman would not know why blacks seem to be more deviant than whites. For all US existence the system has been run for and by the white man. So the laws have been more in favor of the white man despite the 14th amendment, civil rights, and an increased number of blacks legislatures. So I'm supposed to talk about a time when I broke a rule or broke the law.

Using old slavery brer rabbitt reasoning I can say that I've never broken a law in America. Any of my deviant acts are justified by the fact that Mr. Charlie is, was, and will be unfair to people of African descent. So anything we do to survive, get what is rightfully ours anyway—can be justified because of Mr. Charlie's meanness.

That certainly was a far tangent.

On graduation night a policeman stopped me and gave me those drunk driving tests. The irony—I did not drink at all that night, even after the police incident; He stopped me because I WAS swerving like a drunkard; and I was president of our local SADD [Students Against Drunk Driving] chapter.

Here at UT [University of Texas] a policeman made me very upset. It was Monday after Spring Break. We had just come back from a Black baptist Student retreat in Alabama. I was on a spiritual high. But, the policeman almost made me get on his physical head. I had his number and was really ready to call downtown and report that some prejudiced policeman harrassed me. But, I went to my dorm cubicle and read some words from the Living Bible. The words said that the policeman would not reprimand me if I was right. The policeman is there to help us observe the laws etc. That's Bible—not Mr. Charlie. So, of course I took heed and calmed down.

This is an essay replete with ironic tensions, beginning with tension between reader and writer. The writer indirectly criticizes me as a liberal white academic (a "white less bigoted than a Klansman" but bigoted nonetheless) for expecting African-Americans to have a story of deviance to tell. She finds a way to explain, ironically, why she has never been deviant. Then she lets me off the hook, it seems, by calling her chastisement an innocent "tangent."

But I am not off the hook, for my white system of justice, set against a higher justice, is to be examined in two short narratives. Divinity's story about a white policeman stopping a black driver sends out immediate warning signals, as white policemen, especially in the South, are widely known to have harassed African-Americans. This story holds a double irony. Divinity did deserve to be stopped, but for her driving, not intoxication. Although she does not explain this in the essay, she was swerving from fatigue, having been at an all night alcohol- and chemical-free party. That, and the fact that she was president of Students Against Drunk Driving, are the other ironies.

The second incident is evidently a story of real harassment. Again Divinity makes the irony clear by pointing out that she was returning from a religious function. And she clearly sets herself in a position of victory over the bigoted policeman by invoking a higher authority. I suppose she likewise implies that she does not blame me for my blunder, for she was quite cooperative and cheerful in our later interview, and she gave positive and encouraging comments on my first version of this study. In fact, as I have mentioned a number of times, she shared some of her private short story writing with me.

Although this was the most blatant example of signifying on the research, it occurred in other contexts. By this signifying, the informants were able to balance their sometimes conflicting roles as students, informants in a research project, African-Americans, and, in the case of Max and Shanique, research assistants. They were able to maintain a certain distance from the project and to keep from being too closely identified with anything that might do harm to them as African-Americans. They were on their guard against easy labeling that would define them not as University of Texas students but as African-Americans. As Thomas put it, no matter how he tried to succeed in the university, there would always be a feeling that he was there because of Affirmative Action. As he told me,

> I've heard murmurs and things like this when I've been in corridors, like, well, if he does get in it's because the school is stepping down to get him. If he does graduate with honors, maybe he graduated with a 3.0 and not a 3.2. It's just, there's always an undercurrent of, well, we're, you're helping them and because, because they're less than adequate.

This feeling of being singled out because of race is intensified in a setting where, in the vast majority of classes, there is only one African-American student. The inevitable feeling is defensiveness about being different. Thus, informants participating in a study of Black English would feel a need for distance and for control over impressions. Because these informants were aware that my findings would be written up in a doctoral dissertation, and perhaps be published elsewhere, they knew that it would be read by people who would form impressions of them and by extension of all African-Americans. They were not naive enough to believe that these readers would not generalize from them as individuals to their race as a whole. They were aware that minority groups are generally subject to facile stereotyping. They were aware, as African-American academic Bell Hooks has described her own student experience, that their "performance would have future implications for all black students and this knowledge heighten[ed] performance anxiety from the very beginning" (60). To control ultimate impressions of them, they worked to control my immediate impressions.

The pattern of signifying emerged for me as I tried to sort out how they managed their conflicting roles and how they perceived their audience. I found they sometimes made direct comments about the research, their roles, and their audiences that also provided clues.

Two instances of such direct commenting occur in letters, one Divinity's and the other Spike's. Divinity's letter begins with a traditional greeting then explains the situation behind the letter. Since Divinity and this friend normally correspond by sending audio tapes, there is evidently some need to explain a real letter:

> I actually would have sent a tape, but I am being studied by a doctoral candidate who is doing her dissertation on Black English. Now isn't that special? I get five dollars an hour and today I got ten dollars because I refered Dinese to the study. Talk about easy money! Valerie is gona make a copy of this for her study so I won't ask you about any deep dark secrets.

The letter moves on to innocent gossip about boys and parties and the weather. Throughout, Divinity seems aware of the fact that her Black English is being studied; in fact, it may be that she produces "slang" just for my benefit, as in the following example:

> Last night I went to Soul Nite at the Union. David and Tony were there. When I first saw Tony he was dancing with some created being that had on a spandex looking red tight jumpsuit and Bessie-looking high heeled white Prince-James brown type dancing shoes. A sight to see! Now who is truly SOULFUL. Hey, jumpback wanna kiss myself! Girl! I thought the girl was gonna organize a SOUL TRAIN line!

Not only is Divinity using BEV slang here, but she is also signifying on the girl's style, which evidently was too obviously conceited and too stereotypically BLACK. In her signifying on this hapless girl, she is also sending me a clear message about herself and about how I should monitor my perceptions of African-Americans.

In Spike's letter, mention is also made of his role as an informant. Again, the topic seems to arise as a way to explain why Spike is writing since he evidently seldom does:

> Well, man I know this is strange: A letter! (Who writes letters!) First, I'll begin with why I writing a letter! Remember Max Southerland? So you DO! Well he got me to participate in this study of *"Black* English." (I know, what's *"Black* English"? Beats Me!) Anyway she, the

head of the experiment, is studying this letter and some recordings of black conversations.

Like Divinity, Spike is fully aware of his role as an informant and of my role as a researcher. His talk of an "experiment" suggests that he has some image of what the research enterprise entails; furthermore, he may wish to show that he can influence, through his rhetoric, the experiment's outcome. At least, he clearly has a multiple audience in mind for this letter. He pointedly mentions that I will read it. Evidently, I am supposed to overhear his skepticism about "*Black* English." After giving the research as the initial reason for writing, he goes on to more personal reasons for writing (it is cheaper than calling, to give general news, and so on). He apparently ignores my "presence" from this point forward, yet, having been so strongly invoked, I cannot disappear.

It is not unreasonable to speculate that those whose language is continually monitored, whose every gesture and word is judged as somehow indicative of their race and whose race is judged as somehow determining everything about them, would often feel themselves overheard and observed, like informants in a research project. In this respect, my research is a metaphor for their lives. Observation is not a state of being that they can escape, so rather than rebel against the research by not cooperating, they resist it by trying to shape it, partly by letting me know that they know that I am listening, evaluating, and judging. Resistance, if they succeed, will have the positive outcome of influencing our view of African-Americans. Signifying is a subtle style that can accomplish this resistance safely—if resistance is too overt, the consequence might be suppression or further negative stereotyping; if too covert, the message might be missed. Signifying further provides a hedge in that if the message is taken as offensive, it can be denied.

Audiences

As Divinity's and Spike's letters demonstrate, the informants never completely forgot that they were always being overheard when they participated in this research. Far from obtaining natural speech, then, I have collected a corpus of fairly self-conscious attempts to manipulate audience impressions. If we define signifying broadly, as an indirect comment upon another's language or behavior, their linguistic manipulations are significations on the research(er).

For the written essays, there are two audiences whose impressions they work to control: (1) the researcher, who in this case takes on something like the teacher-as-examiner role described by Britton; and (2) the educated general public designated as the audience on the assignment sheet, who in this case includes the eventual readers of the research and who is represented by the researcher. For the letters, the real recipients must be added as the third audience.

For the interviews with me, there are likewise two audiences: (1) the researcher as interviewer; and (2) the eventual readers of the research. But for the interviews with Max and Shanique, the third audience to be added is (3) the research assistant as interviewer.

Differences in status and level of familiarity are influential factors here, but equally influential is whether the audience is known or unknown; that is, whether there is at least some face-to-face contact or other communication that allows a basis for judgment about audience constraints. In this regard, the eventual readers of the research, the "educated general public," must be completely fictionalized by the speakers/writers. Their novice status as academic writers makes an understanding of the loaded term "educated" quite difficult. However, it seems fairly clear that as African-American informants, they are concerned with this "mainstream" group's image of blacks.

Similarly, my own role as researcher must be fictionalized to some degree, since it is not exactly the familiar role of teacher-as-examiner. There is always the question of what the researcher is looking for and the related question of how to control what the researcher finds. This is an especially important question for these informants, for they are already grappling with emerging identities. As freshmen and sophomores, they are learning to become college students; furthermore, as African-Americans they are trying to avoid stereotyping by both their African-American peers and by the larger academic community. They do not want to be seen as "oreos," white inside and black outside, nor do they want to be judged as being coddled by Affirmative Action. At any rate, the informants must do their best to decide how to play to me as researcher by imagining what the researcher role requires. The example from Divinity's essay given above reveals that she has cast me at least partially as a "well-meaning but somewhat ignorant white liberal." And Spike evidently sees me in somewhat clinical terms, though his stance is more bemused than respectful.

Polo, Thomas, Spike, Laurie, Dinese, and Divinity have to alter somewhat their usual relationship with Max and Shanique, if only because of the presence of the tape recorder. Although they seem at ease with this audience, they certainly remember that Max and Shanique are working for that invisible presence who will later listen to their words. Thus, we can expect some impression management to continue even in this most relaxed situation. Peer loyalties tend to win out in these sorts of situations, of course, so if any signifying is to be done, it will most likely be done at the expense of the research itself (and by extension the researcher and the extended audience she represents).

Balancing Roles: Researcher, Informant, African-American, and Student

The informants have a number of roles available to them in relation to these audiences. For example, they can construct the role of research assistant (in the case of Max and Shanique), informant in a research project, African-American (and thus representative of BEV speakers), or university student. Using Le Page's and Tabouret-Keller's model, we might assume that they work from their stereotypes of a given role and model their language and behaviors (though here I am concerned only with language) to show that they fit those stereotypes. Again, when we conceive of signifying broadly, this sort of impression management can be seen as an instance of signification.

Let me use Max as an example. To show he is a good student, he talks "intelligently" and "formally" using what he perceives to be the sort of words good students should use. Likewise, to construct the ethos of a good informant, he is attentive and cooperative and occasionally produces BEV slang (since he generally associates BEV itself with slang). To construct the ethos of a good research assistant, he talks "seriously" about the topic under study, BEV, to show that he has knowledge about it. And he asks questions designed to steer his interviewees to discuss this topic, even though I do not explicitly ask him to do so. Finally, to combat negative stereotypes of African-American males or of BEV speakers, he portrays himself as intelligent, hardworking, serious, religious, and responsible. He takes pains to show that his English is good and that he has conscious control over his use of BEV slang. Furthermore, he occasionally uses slang to demonstrate his allegiance to African-American culture.

Within a given social situation we may sometimes select and sometimes be assigned roles, which we perform in ways that allow us to construct a desired ethos. In constructing a front (or ethos), Goffman claims, we attempt to gain a measure of control over others by defining the situation in which interaction occurs. For example, if Max successfully constructs the ethos of a good research assistant during his interview with Spike, Spike must either decide to go along and play a good informant or attempt to redefine the situation by somehow undermining Max's ethos and constructing a counter ethos, perhaps that of a poor informant who wants to confound the study by not cooperating with the research assistant. He might even be so successful as to convince Max to switch to the role of a poor research assistant. Actually, Max successfully constructs the ethos of a good researcher, and no informant attempts to alter his definition of the situation.

Max plays the role of research assistant primarily when he interviews others for me, though this role may influence his behavior in other contexts. Commonly, however, when Max plays research assistant, I play researcher, and he and I are on the same team. As teammates, we work together to control our audience's impressions. We are insiders, while those we study and those who will read the results are audience members. We project a front—we are serious and competent researchers collecting data about bidialectal BEV speakers. We even have props: consent forms, biographical data sheets, a tape recorder, blue exam books, payment for services, and an office on campus. It matters a great deal to both of us that our audience believes our projected front. I want the participants to cooperate so that they do not distort the data, while Max wants them to uphold his projection of himself as a

good assistant, and ultimately his image of himself as a competent African-American male and BEV speaker. I want the readers
of the study to respect my work, while Max wants to convince
them that all African-American males and all BEV speakers
deserve respect.

Max seems to understand that constructing the ethos of a
competent research assistant requires that he elicit as much discourse as he can from the interviewees and that to do so he must
put them at ease. He convinces me that he takes the assistant role
seriously. For one thing, he is vitally interested in the topic of
Black English and obviously feels it is worth studying. He introduces it into every interview and reports to me that he has discussed it with friends; he is curious about how to define it and
eager to learn as much as he can about it. For another thing, in the
field notes he writes that his behavior is purposely geared toward
eliciting data: "I feel that we as interviewers must comment and
talk in order to put the interviewees at ease." And finally, I see
that he feels a sense of importance connected with being my assistant. In his interview with Thomas, for example, he asks about the
significance of their contribution to the study of Black English:

Max: What do you feel about the Black English issue itself? How will this
documentary, this, I mean, uh, this conversation help to, uh, I
dunno, kind of create a Whack English (*laughs*) White and Black, just
to combine [unintelligible word]
Thomas: How do I feel Black English will?
Max: Well, no, I mean, all the efforts that are being made now, with the
taping and things like that. What do you think could be learned from,
uh, . . . (*Thomas, taking advantage of the pause, interrupts with a
long answer.*)

Although he laughs at his creation, *Whack English*, his use of the
word *documentary* betrays both his sense that he is participating
in serious work and that he is consciously performing the role of
research assistant. Whether Max finally is sincere in playing this
role is impossible to judge.

A good instance of Max's success as a research assistant
occurs in his rather difficult interview with Thomas, difficult
because Thomas, after using BEV with Max, confesses that he considers BEV a "joke" and that he only uses it because he feels pressure from his African-American peers to confirm solidarity with
them. This puts Max in an awkward position. He could lose face

because Thomas' confession might cause him to break character, to show anger or dissent, which would harm the cool, intelligent, and harmonious ethos of the African-American male he wishes to construct. He cannot agree that BEV is a joke, since he has made it clear that he does not believe this, yet he cannot allow himself to challenge Thomas and run the risk of having to concede that African-American males bully one another into using an inferior dialect because they feel insecure. Furthermore, Max is faced with a problem as a research assistant, for by angering Thomas he risks losing his cooperation in the interview. His solution shows his skill as a diplomat and as a researcher, for he in fact clarifies Thomas' views of BEV to discover if they are indeed as negative as they sound. In the passage reproduced below, Max's delivery is calm and deliberate:

Max: That's interesting because we haven't really touched on, uh, it being a feeling of force to speak Black English, and, uh, that's a interesting point. So you actually feel you have to speak in a certain way when you're around, uh, black brothers and sisters?

Thomas: Yeah, I feel like I have to defer a little bit as far as my own strengths for Standard English. I have to defer a little bit and give and take in the situation, giving meaning, uh, the Black English, you know, and the take, like, you know, just make my Standard English submissive and just back off, just a little bit, you know. You just, you just can't go up, you know, into these black groups like an A Fie A meeting and go, "Well, well, I feel that this is not, you know, a consequential action that will, you know, be such as, you know, to be in reference to this." If you say something like that you've, you've already got blackballed. You could see the look in their eyes, you know, it's just, it's like, "Well, where'd we get white bread from?" (*Max laughs*). . . . I mean anyone who's brought up in that kind of environment can tell when things are not going over so well . . . I don't have to behave like that, so why should I? It's a problem.

Max: Exactly. Tell me something. What type of environment did you grow up in? I mean, did you grow up in a black environment or, I know you went to a predominantly white high school.

Thomas: Yeah.

Max: So, uh, how did that compensate for your being able to communicate, you know, with a black society?

Thomas goes on to explain that he learned BEV outside his home, where his parents had taught him that it was improper English. Then he discusses his high school experience:

I was a black man in a white man's environment, and they, most ah the black people I met there, at school, felt like I should, you know, push aside the white environment and hold on strongly to the black ideas. And, this kind of thing. Which included Black English. I don't know where that throws, that gets thrown in as being part of blackness, but it, you know, it is.

A long dialogue on this topic follows, prompting Max finally to say sympathetically:

Max: Well the key thing that I see is, (*aside*) here it is turn, turning into (*laughs*) Dr. Ruth. (*both laugh*) I mean it all comes back to being yourself. You have to assert yourself to be as comfortable as you can, you know. And with your faith in God and everything, he'll allow you to, uh, learn from the experiences that you have had and to be able to be more comfortable with yourself and, uh, I found that even you talking to me sometimes, you know, we get black with each other.

Thomas: Yeah.

Max: But then we can talk intellectual also. But because the mentality of us being black, I find it, you know, you find yourself more or most of the time relating to me in black dialect. You know. It's just because it just seems like that's the way it's supposed to be. But it's not really, you know, a necessary thing.

Max has avoided accusation yet still has pointed out that Thomas does speak to him in BEV. But he puts the best face on it, venturing a guess that it improves their informal relations. He even uses humor, joking about his role as interviewer, which eases the tension and allows him to give unsolicited advice.

Max also successfully plays the role of informant. Interestingly, in his interview with Spike he even labels himself as an informant, showing that he has accepted it as a role identity:

And, uh, the interesting thing, you know, that she has expressed to me is that we, as her subjects, are able to, you know, communicate with both black individuals and white individuals.

As an informant, Max has clearly set out to influence his audience's impression not only of himself but of all African-American males, deliberately using the study as a forum to air his own and his peers' views on being, as he jokingly phrases it "a black man in a white man's world." He frequently brings up the special problems of African-American males, using the taping and his writing as an opportunity to construct an ethos of the African-American male that will defeat some of the stereotypes that properly offend him. The future readers of the study are obviously the audience he most wants to reach, but to do so he must first create the correct impression for me.

Thus we see that this role of informant, as well as the roles of African-American and student, change the configurations of our relationships. I find myself in a new role, the audience to a routine performed by Max and his fellow participants; he finds them cooperative, probably without having to discuss the matter, since they seem to share an agenda. If they didn't, they would not be likely to participate in the study in the first place. At any rate, all the males showed signs of sharing Max's sense that this study could indeed be used as a vehicle for improving the image of the African-American male. For example, during Max's interview with Polo, negative stereotypes of African-American males becomes a topic:

Polo: Man, that's why brothers like us have to try so hard to dispel the stereotype we have. (*laughs*)
Max: Yes.
Polo: Of boofin' every babe we can. (*laughs*)
Max: Yes. It's, it's bad.
Polo: Shit, man.
Max: But it's the truth 'cause the babes are even set to the pattern.

They see this study as an avenue for overcoming this unflattering and ill-fitting image of the African-American male. By indirect hints, i.e., signification, they chip away at this unjust stereotype.

Max consistently has shown interest in the image of the African-American male. He wrote a paper on that topic in his freshman English class, almost eight months before this study, and the topic comes up as a concern over and over again in his interviews. For example, in discussing BEV with me (a topic which he, incidentally, introduced), he brings up African-American identity:

Throughout history, I mean, from the beginning of the slave trade and stuff like that, we have been thought of as ignorant. . . . Blacks have been thought of as ignorant. . . . You know, it's, habits are hard to break. And so throughout history we still have this misidentity. Our culture and everything is just misidentified.

Here he makes explicit his view of African-American identity: blacks have been unjustly stereotyped as ignorant.

As the conversation progresses, he brings up the identity of African-American males more specifically. In the next excerpt, he is describing *American Pictures*, a slide show:

Max: It was a bunch of slides, and it just showed the poverty that blacks face and the problems that we've gone through the years up to the present day and how there's still slavery, you know, and such as share cropping, how that was used, that's the same thing as wh-, welfare, and different things like crutches that blacks have to lean on because for the black male (*laughs*) society have no, society has no place for 'em. And that's why since [unintelligible word] time, I mean, they tried to break us. When we came over from slavery because the African family was so strong, and they knew that to break the father would create turmoil. And, it worked . . . so a lot of people were broken. Yeah, so we still trying to, we're still trying to gain our identity. And it's really . . .
Valerie: How do you see that struggle going?
Max: It's, it's not really going.

The African-American male, broken by the history of slavery and the attempts by his dominators to keep him down, is left to rebuild his identity and his pride. Interestingly, in this speech Max revises his own language, changing from BEV to SAE when he says "society have no, society has no place for 'em" and, ironically, "So we still trying to, we're still trying to gain our identity," making the point that gaining identity is connected with how we present ourselves through language.

Sometimes the informants refer jokingly to being black men. Notice how in the excerpt below from Max's interview with Spike, Max initiates the topic of the black man, and Spike takes it up:

Spike: God! Why do they make you take courses they know could kill you, man. I could [unintelligible word] God! I could, I could be a happy man, let's put it that way, at the end of the semester.
Max: A happy black man.
Spike: I could be a (*laughs loudly*) happy black man! But I'll probably be a pretty sad black man, depending on calculus.

Simply by calling themselves black they seem to be showing me, and the readers of my study, that they identify themselves as African-American men and that they are conscious of being studied because of this identity.

Furthermore, they seem to want to make a point about being

African-American. As the conversation continues, the topic of blackness reoccurs as an underlying theme. Max moves the discussion from school to Black English, and from there they go on to interracial friendships and dating and their perception of the lack of racial prejudice in the military and in ROTC. This leads to a discussion of success in business and back to African-American identity:

Spike: You've got to prove that you've got actually something more than that little degree in business 'cause it really just doesn't mean a whole lot, 'specially if you're black.
Max: Um hum.
Spike: 'Cause when you go out there, that's when the racism is.

And then they consider the obligation of African-American businessmen (which Spike aspires to be) to, as Max puts it, "change the, uh, racial tension that, uh, exists today." A graphic illustration of the focus of their discussion on African-American identity comes when Max turns the tape over. In an altered voice, taking on the role of a talk show host, he announces: "We are now breaking to, ah, reverse the tape to the other side, and we will continue our discussion on the black male in society today." Clearly, Max is letting me, the covert audience, in on the action. We can assume that he is also attempting to control my impressions to some degree, by focusing my attention on a particular topic.

Max and the other males perform yet another routine, meant to influence how I, and by extension the readers of this book, see speakers of BEV. All of the informants are singled out by me as special because they are bidialectal and can speak BEV, but none of them are entirely comfortable with this role. Although they never tell me so directly, I believe they wish to retain control over my view of BEV, so that I do not misunderstand what it means to be a BEV speaker and, by extension, so that I do not misreport it. Max describes himself in his interview with Thomas as a competent bidialectal:

I personally grew up in an entirely black environment, and I have been mixed into white situations where I can communicate, you know, with a white person if I had to or an intellectual conversation if, uh, it would be the case, but I'm used to being in an all black environment, and, you know, that's just it's nor-, more normal for me to talk in slang and hip hop hippity hop hop thing, you know. (*Thomas laughs*) But (*laughs*) it's not (*laughs*) a necessary type thing.

Max marks himself here as having special knowledge, which is, of course, true. What interests me, however, is his choice of the word "intellectual" in this context. I believe he is anxious to show that he can communicate in an intellectual manner and that he is aware that BEV is not generally considered appropriate for such discourse.

Essentially, the females in this study, like the males, are subverting our stereotypes through signification, although their doing so may be less a concerted effort. Shanique, by virtue of the smart talking ethos she constructs (discussed in Chapter 5), shows us that African-American women, even those who speak BEV, are not all welfare mothers. In their own ways, her friends participate in this demonstration. Laurie is concerned with being seen as a lady and as an intelligent and politically aware student and future businesswoman (see Chapter 6). Divinity and Dinese show themselves to be politically aware honor students with professional ambitions. Divinity plans to be a writer and Dinese a lawyer. While their use of BEV and their attitudes towards its proper use differ slightly, all of them show respect for it and for its speakers. Even though they do not bring up the topic of language as frequently and as persistently as the males, they are quite aware of their roles as informants in a study of BEV and are aware as well that they represent BEV speakers to those who will read the study results.

Like Max, Shanique has the most demands on her to balance various roles. As a research assistant, she is on my performance team, and as an informant and student she is on the same team as the other participants. It is interesting to examine how Shanique manages these roles. Although she mentions her studies often and her future plans to be a doctor even more, Shanique does not seem as engaged as Max does with the student role. However, she convinces me that she is a serious scholar. For example, she indicates a number of times that she does not want to be distracted from studying. She writes in her letter that she chose to end a conversation with an attractive male to go to class: "As usual I had to end my happiness by being the good little girl I am and went to class." Generally, she seems to invoke the student role only enough to ensure that she will be taken seriously. I have every reason (including her grades) to believe that her presentation of herself in this respect is sincere.

She also acts out the role of research assistant rather differently than does Max, taking my instructions more at face value. Unlike Max, she does not try to collect information specifically on BEV, nor does she refer to the questions I give her for ideas. But like Max, she does an admirable job of putting her interviewees at ease and initiating informal and comfortable conversation. In fact, she performs the role of assistant exactly as I had instructed, except that she talks rather more than a good field worker would be expected to talk. Her chattering may be a strategy she employs as a member of my team. For talkative Shanique, such behavior is quite natural, and I did tell her above all else to be natural. That she is actually using this as a strategy seems quite possible to me, for I myself tried it, though less successfully, in my first interview with Laurie. I assumed that by talking at length myself, for example telling stories about times I had faced danger, I would put the informants at ease and prompt reciprocation. Whether because of or in spite of my talking, Laurie was fairly comfortable. She told Shanique, "When I was talking to Valerie I just took off my shoes." But, unfortunately, I found myself with a tape that gave me as much data on myself as on Laurie. Max, as he indicates in his field notes (quoted above), also uses this technique of talking at length to put his interviewees at ease.

In spite of Shanique's loquaciousness, which in the long run is an asset since she is a primary informant, she displays real talent as a research assistant as regards my instructions to be as inconspicuous as possible with the recorder. For example, Laurie did not even notice her turn it on when they started their interview. As the tape starts, they are laughing and chatting. Suddenly Shanique says:

Shanique: Yeah, I've already turned it on. I see you looking over there, looking all suspicious and stuff, so, uh, I'ma put my foot up. I, I got to get comfortable. I have long legs.
Laurie: I see. My goodness.
Shanique: I got to stretch 'em. Like my shoes?
Laurie: I seen those shoes before, chile.
Shanique: Oh! Well, um, I went to get the tickets.

By acknowledging Laurie's suspicious look, Shanique defuses her curiosity and finds a way to move her attention progressively from the recorder to putting her feet up (an invitation to relax) to new shoes. Laurie's reaction to Shanique's shoes indicates that Shanique is simply trying to change the topic of conversation. Shanique's hesitant reply ("Oh! Well, um . . .") suggests she has been buying time, looking for a new topic, finally settling on tickets to the basketball game, which they go on to discuss at great length.

A similar incident occurs with Divinity, who is a particularly challenging subject because of her rather sharp awareness of the recorder. But Shanique, as this passage shows, handles her quite easily:

Divinity: Oh! The thing is on?
Shanique: Yeah.
Divinity: I didn't know it was on. I was going to say, when you going to turn it on?
Shanique: I'm slick, I'm good.
Divinity: I saw you do it! I looked right at it, but I didn't . . .
Shanique: You didn't see it?
Divinity: I think I was looking here, and I didn't know if you really turned it on, or if you just fiddled with it.
Shanique: Oh.
Divinity: Got my name all on the tape!
Shanique: Um hum. Make you look like you're important.
Divinity: Um hum. Spelled it right and everything. I guess I am. (*both laugh*)
Shanique: Oh, she needs to get your schedule.
Divinity: Okay.

Divinity, talking about her schedule as she writes it out, gets into a discussion of time management and classes, and finally begins to talk about a trip to Alabama. At least for a time, the recorder is forgotten. Shanique has enhanced her ethos (she is "slick" in Dinese's eyes and "good" as a researcher in mine). By acting cool and natural, she defuses Divinity's attention. If she had instead challenged Divinity, told her to divert her attention or tried too conspicuously to divert it, she only would have made Divinity suspicious. She employs the delicate art of indirection to manipulate Divinity.

Later in the interview, Divinity's attention is again suddenly drawn to the recorder. In the middle of a conversation about men and matchmaking, Divinity says:

Divinity: Oooo! This thing got a telephone hook-up.
Shanique: Yeah. I was, I was trying to figure out what I could do (*laughs*) with that.
Divinity: Really.

Shanique: But her telephone won't come out. I mean, the cord on her telephone won't come out. I was trying to, shoot, I was just getting inquisitive, discover something.

Divinity: Girl! Trace the, well, you wouldn't trace the call, but you sure would have them people's words.

Shanique: Uh huh. Be serious.

Divinity: Um. No, cause I, I, he's been around me enough to know.

And Divinity returns to the previous topic. Again, Shanique stays cool, even herself admits complicity and curiosity about the telephone hook-up on the recorder, but finally brings Divinity back to the topic with her gently spoken "Be serious," which is more in the nature of agreement than admonishment and which indicates closure for that topic. Thus, we can see that Shanique has not forgotten her role as a research assistant and is quite aware that she is required to elicit informal conversation and to keep attention diverted from the recorder as much as possible. She remains a faithful member of the research team, but she balances that role with the role of fellow informant.

One final incident with Divinity is interesting because Shanique handles it so differently from the way I imagine Max would. Shanique evidently picks up from my desk a photocopied article on Black English:

Divinity: What is that?

Shanique: It's about black language. She got it out of a book, and I was going to read it.

Divinity: Black what?

Shanique: Language.

Divinity: Oh.

Shanique: It was, somebody did a, something black on white.

Divinity: Um.

Shanique: (*reads*) "The Story of English."

Divinity: I tripped out when I found out that was what it was. The question said "What, what do, what do you think of Black English?" And I, I did, I never thought about it. You know, I was just like, I kind of think I knew what it was but the question was what was tripping me out. I was like, what? Sort of a strange question. (*Shanique laughs*) Hmmm.

Shanique: I don't know. Have you seen Max?

Divinity: Um hum. He had a test today.

Curiously, Shanique does not pursue the topic of BEV as Max undoubtedly would have. Nor does she let the incident get out of hand. It seems that this is a situation where Shanique's roles as research assistant and informant are at odds. As a member of my team, she can lose face if she ridicules my question about Black English, perhaps undermining the data as well as her performance as my assistant. However, as an informant, she is a member of Divinity's team, and Divinity has shown just enough suspicion to indicate that she is testing Shanique to find out if I am to be trusted. Rather than play either role, Shanique changes the topic.

The informants use signifying as a major resource to achieve impression management. Sometimes their signifying is fairly obvious, at other times less so. They may bring up particular topics (like Black English or "black man in a white man's world") or use language (such as slang or fancy or smart talk) calculated to have an effect or make a point. By this means, they notify me that they are on their guard against facile or racist stereotyping. They even educate me in some ways, especially Divinity, as when she comments on the Soul Train stereotype or the white liberal who expects deviance. But their suspicions are not so great that they refuse to participate in the study. Certainly the reason isn't "easy money," for they earn very little by helping me. I would guess that their cooperative spirit comes from their belief that this research represents an opportunity to show their strengths and to combat ignorance. They are confident that their words will come across well, that they will be perceived as intelligent, even eloquent, and as well-versed in the English language as any of their peers.

Talking
and Writing
with High Style

Bartholomae has made the powerful suggestion that college students undergo a process of "inventing" the university by progressively approximating the conventions and ethos of academic discourse. Because of their unfamiliarity with academic writing, students must invent its special terminology, cadences, arguments, and commonplaces. They must write as if they were already academics, with the knowledge and authority of experts, and to do so, Bartholomae suggests, they become mimics ("Inventing the University"; see also Shaughnessy 45). He does not tell us much about how they accomplish this mimicry, other than that they establish roles for themselves, such as "researcher" or "professor" and play them out as best they can. But he suggests that the student playing researcher has some idea of how a researcher writes a report and that the student playing professor has a vision of how a professor explicates a poem. Certainly we can conclude that these students have some stereotypical model for academic discourse (or, as Bartholomae points out, discourses, since academic discourse varies with such factors as field or genre). All their stereotypes cannot come from the same source, from television or from previous schooling, for example. However, it is likely that all of them represent some prestigious form of discourse, something they can identify as educated and formal.

The general theory of Le Page and Tabouret-Keller can be of help here. One tries to approximate the language of the group with which he or she wishes to be identified. I repeat their theory once more:

> The individual creates for himself the patterns of his linguistic behaviour so as to resemble those of the group or groups with which from time to time he wishes to be identified, or so as to be unlike those from whom he wishes to be distinguished. (181)

Students wish to be identified with the university community, and their instructors expect them to write as if they were. Thus, their attempts to write, especially their most naive productions, will reflect their stereotypes of academic discourse.

In this chapter, it will be seen that the academic writing of Max, Polo, and Thomas is influenced by African-American rhetoric. In their attempt to appropriate formal, academic discourse, they draw upon their repertoire of language strategies, a repertoire which includes, although it is not limited to, African-American rhetoric. Because of associated prestige, they draw upon witty verbal performance in general and upon fancy talk and the African-American homiletic tradition in particular.

These young men are striving to be identified with the university. This creates some conflict for them, insofar as it may be perceived as an attempt to disassociate themselves from African-American culture. Thus, as I discussed in Chapter 1, the process of appropriating academic language for these students is not exactly of the same nature as it is for students not defined by difference. However, I am not claiming that they are in a completely unique position. Formal and ceremonial language as a model for academic discourse is not exclusive to African-Americans. We often hear non-BEV speaking student writers (not to mention professors) break into fancy, grandiose flights of "rhetoric." Like these African-American students, they are attempting to be identified with educated or sometimes literary language by using features stereotypically associated with it. Their stereotypes quite naturally will come from discourse they perceive as elevated or prestigious. They concoct a discourse with borrowings from former teachers, preachers, TV evangelists, and the local mayor; in short, from whatever in their world represents for them respected or formal or educated-sounding language. Still, Max, Thomas, and Polo, I believe, have models for formal discourse that are not available to students who speak only SAE, namely, fancy talk and the African-American homiletic tradition and, to a lesser extent, signifying and other forms of verbal art that carry covert prestige.

As I explained in the last chapter, Max is adept at the appropriation of a number of roles besides that of university student. In each case—student, informant, research assistant, and African-American male—he strives through his language to construct the ethos of a good performer. To the extent that he succeeds, he does so partly by modeling his language to conform to stereotypes he identifies with these roles. Yet to some extent, notably in his academic writing and perhaps with some audiences for his speaking, he fails to construct the intended educated ethos. To clarify how and why he fails, we have to examine the stereotypes he holds for each role to which he aspires and how he models his language to show his identity with these roles. We must also examine the cultural expectations surrounding each role. We can surmise that the model for "intelligent" or "serious" speech depends upon cultural factors. What Max thinks makes him sound intelligent in an academic essay may differ from what I think would make him sound intelligent. Max attempts to construct a respectable, intellectual ethos suitable for formal or semi-formal academic discourse by talking proper, which, of course, insofar as it means speaking in grammatically correct SAE, serves him well. But he also models himself on the witty and intelligent man-of-words by talking fancy, and this, in an academic context, sometimes works against him. Unfortunately, not yet being a master at the game of adapting fancy talk for a non-BEV speaking audience, and, not yet able to use BEV forms, as we see Bishop Cleveland do so artfully in his sermons, he uses fancy talk for the wrong audience in the wrong context, and he even tends to overdo it. Instead of intellectual, he may appear, to some academics at least, insincere; instead of fluent, he may appear clumsy.

The reason Max may not come off well when he employs fancy talk has much to do with our theories of style. Most handbooks and style books eschew rhetorical embellishment of the sort valued in African-American fancy talk. Diction considered appropriate for academic discourse is usually standard, reasonably current (no archaic words or neologisms), and national (foreign words being limited to a short list of usually Latin clichés like "et al.," "post hoc," and "vice versa"), concise (avoiding circumlocution), and plain (not euphemistic, pompous, or fancy). *The Little, Brown Handbook* (fourth edition) claims that "Good writers choose their words for their exactness and economy. Pretentious writers choose them in the belief that fancy words will impress readers. They rarely will" (Fowler and Aaron 463). Such a statement might surprise many students, especially those who have strong cultural preferences for styles like fancy talk, yet it quite accurately describes the taste of most college English instructors.

The *Heath Handbook* is equally prescriptive on this matter of style:

Pretentious diction, like the pretentious person, is stiff and phony—in short, a bore. Our diction becomes pretentious if we always choose the polysyllabic word over the word of one syllable, a Latinate word where an Anglo-Saxon one will do, flowery phrases in place of common nouns and verbs. Writing should be as honest and forthright as plain speech. . . . Sometimes, ordinary words seem inadequate to carry the weight we want our thoughts to have, so we decorate statements with ornate language. (Mulderig and Elsbree 249)

This passage reflects two influential theories of style, both of which contribute to a devaluation of fancy talk. The first is best expressed by the opening sentence, that is, that "Pretentious diction, like the pretentious person, is stiff and phony—in short, a bore." Take this statement one step further and you might conclude that pretentious diction is produced by a pretentious person. This is the doctrine that "style is the man," that style expresses character, and it remains highly influential in composition pedagogy. From this perspective, the African-Americans who use fancy talk are simply pretentious or bombastic or insincere. The second view of style reflected here is the classical one—that style is an ornament to thought. From the strictly Aristotelian perspective, the best style is the moderate one that never detracts from a sober and deliberate consideration of facts but that remains appropriate to the rhetorical situation; ideally, style approaches a mean between the extremes of baldly clear and poetically embellished. From this perspective, the African-American fancy talker has a poor sense of the appropriate and tends to embellish with an excess of ornament.

Neither because of a lack of sincerity nor because of obfuscation, but because of community standards, fancy talk is immensely out of place within the context of an academic essay, as would be many of the rhetorical embellishments of the African-American sermon. We have seen that a rhetorical form such as the sermon may be incorporated successfully into a new context, such as political speechmaking or teaching style (Davis; Fine). However, we should remember that successful incorporation is sensitive to many factors of what we might call the performance context, the actors, the audience, the setting, the occasion, the genre, and so on.

That is the down side, but there is an up side. It is represented by such master orators as Dr. Martin Luther King, Jr. or Jesse Jackson or Bishop Cleveland (whose sermons have been analyzed by Davis). These orators have been able to transcend the color barrier and to walk the fine line between approved discourse for both the African-American culture and the culture at large. Granted, the more diverse the audience, the less use there will be of BEV variants or the more extravagant features of fancy talk (malapropism, neologism, or foreign words, for example). Yet their style remains uniquely African-American. There are strategies that Max is at least familiar with that could certainly enhance his academic writing. I believe that he is aware of this and that he tries to draw on these strategies, albeit not always successfully. But, with time, practice, and revision, he could produce written work all the stronger because of the value he places on verbal wit and on talking well.

Some African-American Models for Academic Discourse

Within the BEV discourse community, talking well occurs in two contexts, the secular and the sacred. The secular strain is humorous, playful, full of bravado and challenge; the sacred is serious, formal, ritualized, and poetic. Both strains are heard, acknowledged, and understood by all who participate in the BEV community. Thus, although Max may not explicitly use the term *fancy talk* in the sense I use it here, he certainly hears and understands fancy talk itself within the BEV community. While he is an active church member, he isn't a street kid. However, he does not have to be a street kid to be influenced by street culture. It is pervasive in the community. It is embedded in the language of the culture's rich folkloric tradition. Even as African-Americans like Max, Thomas, and Polo move into middle and upper classes they are influenced by folkloric tradition.

Through his discourse Max reveals the influence of the sacred strain. I was fortunate to hear firsthand a sample of African-American preaching, which I believe he incorporates into his stereotype of academic discourse, when his Gospel choir, Innervisions of Blackness, performed at an Austin church in May, 1987. During the service, the preacher improvised a prayer to dedicate the choir's new robes. This performance was caught on tape (the singing was being taped for sale). As he began to pray, the choir was finishing a rendition of "I Have Decided to Follow Jesus." The preacher's language reflects the typical discourse of the African-American homiletic tradition, which is recognized and respected by all Church members and, I contend, imitated by Max as a model of a respectable and formal discourse. Notice the highly formalized and stylized diction of the prayer:

As the Pharisees render service, but service with a contrite heart, a sincere desire to let those of their peers know that you are real. Because you are in their life, and you have made a difference in them. And today they're representing you. Now, father, You anoint them. Father, You bless them. Let them be an impact in this community and then let it spread abroad. For so many are lost. But there are those here who are lifting up the bloodstained banner. Thank you, Jesus. Thank you, Jesus. And we can't do that without You. We can't even sing without You. We can't even live a life of righteousness without You. So now You bless us, not as man blesses but from shining glory. You bless us. And we'll be forever so mindful, to give You the praise. And remember that all good things come from You. Now, father, these robes that we are wearing today, it is like the shield of faith that You told us to arm ourselves with. It is like the breastplate of righteousness, to quench the fiery darts of the enemy. It is like the helmet of salvation that separates us and lets the world know that there's a difference between holiness and unholiness, clean and unclean, righteousness and unrighteousness. And it is also a reminder to us that we are a peculiar people, peculiar in the sense of being called out. Unique in the sense of being dedicated, inspired, and motivated to be those that will carry the lantern to the width and the breadth and the depth of this world. That's what these robes symbolize. And that each person when they recognize this, that we are not only [unintelligible] they recognize us as being not only members of this organization but as children of God. For we have decided. Not by being forced to. Not because of any works that we have done. Not because we've had to. Not because of trial or tribulation. But out of a free will spirit. We have decided to follow You. Now these are the blessings we ask in Your name, Jesus. Amen. And Amen.

The preacher uses what Polo calls "big words" to enhance the impression that he is speaking from the power of the Spirit: "render"; "impact"; "quench"; "a peculiar people"; "dedicated, inspired, and motivated"; "free will spirit"; and so on. Furthermore, he uses the words in unusual and startling ways, the better to convey his message. For example, "to let those of their peers" seems an odd construction and an odd word to use with the Biblical "Pharisees." He makes an impressive show with metaphor by relating the real robes to the spiritual "shield of faith," "breastplate of righteousness," and "helmet of salvation." Also inspiring to his audience must be his singling them out as a "peculiar" or chosen people. Besides the rather common but effective rhetorical use of parallel structure, the preacher draws on stock phrases like "width and breadth and depth" and "trial and tribulation." "Free will spirit" calls attention to itself as an unusual phrase. Finally, he masterfully weaves in the refrain of the song he had interrupted, "We Have Decided to Follow Jesus," which will continue as he finishes his last amen. In short, though we certainly recognize this prayer as a standard production for an African-American preacher (Davis), with obvious Biblical allusions and language, we can also recognize it as related to the tea meeting speeches of the Caribbean (Chapter 1), which are meant to "confuse" and "amaze" the audience, though in the case of the prayer, the confusion is meant to awe the audience with religious feeling.

I can hear strains of this ritualized, formalized language in Max's essay on Black English, especially in the conclusion:

> The question of Black English has brought much attention to the ever increasing problems Blacks face as a race. Is it bad English or is it a sign of ignorance to speak Black dialect? Because of this question, I am left to wonder if it is only because of racial difference that a problem exist. We as a black race have been shifted from all moral or ethical reality of our own identities. This is because of our unfit place in the white society we live in.
>
> It is true that a person who speaks only Black English is at a disadvantage in this society. However, this society only refers to the American capitalistic, white oriented society, (ACWOS). The same statement is false in most environments where Blacks have been placed and forced by the (ACWOS), to remain. These places are the ghetto's. Instead of getting rid of ghetto's complitely, society only rebuilds them. Thus there are two different worlds that have been created through histories mean punch in America, the white and the Black world. We will now focus in on the Black world were the problem of communication seems to arise.
>
> The black world has been shunned for many deep scared years. Forced to remain silent and forced to exist with out an education for the greater part of their lives, Blacks have had to create their own median of communication. Whether it be through song, music,

dance, weeping, church, or family unity and love, Blacks have mananged to escape their silent punishment and have created their own way of expressing themselves to each other. Because Blacks were stolen from their native land, Africa, their native culture, their native tongue, and their native people, their exist an excuse for the ignorance they possessed and have not yet grown out of to the unfamiliarity of the with language and customs.

In the modern ghetto Blacks are not custom to fine education and many never see white faces. Therefore, a language they could call their own was developed, redefined, and molded to a comfortable way of espressing day to day troubles, desires, ambitions, and needs. This language, though not understood by the majority of the white society, is a source of identity for the Black race, the Black World. An identity that has been lost, stolen or astray for years that seem to be inumerable or uncountable. However, even this identity seems to trouble society. Society feels that Black English is an ignorant language when it may as well be the cause of Black ignorance. Placed in ghetto prisans and unrealistic poverty conditions of hunger, fear and disgust, how is a productive, middle class, well rounded, and educated individual expected to be grown. Those conditions are only shaping survivalist, hard and stern individuals who have no family encouragement to assist them through school. Most ghetto youth have no families and are left to beat a system that has long ago deemed unbeatable.

I myself am able to communicate with my Black brothers and sisters in what has been proclaimed, "Black English," because these are the people I have grown up with and have become used to. Though I did not grow up in a ghetto, as a Black youth I have been crippled by societies ghetto mentality. This mentality stereotypes me too as unfit to make it in a properly unbroken English spoken world. I have been educated and have realized that my writing is a tool to express feelings otherwise hushed or shuned by society. Poetry being many Black's ticket to open protest, I have compassed an outright, however limited view of the moral debasement and silent awakening of the Black race.

In conclusion, the Black race has only the abilities to catch up to the white races advancements at our own speed and no doubt with the aid of our white brothers and societies. The question that exist in the annals of my mind now is, When will we reach that golden day when color will no longer be a factor, when speech will be a unified body in America as well as unity amongst all races, and when Black and white English will no longer represent a seperate Black and White world and will be associated with a peaceful united term Whack English?

Max's effort is certainly that of a novice, writing under time pressure, but it also reveals some strengths of expression that hint at his use of the African-American sermon as a model. He makes sophisticated use of parallel sentence structure, as, for example, in paragraph three; the same paragraph illustrates his ability with subordinate sentence patterns. He displays a preference for the rhetorical question (paragraphs one, and four, and six), and he invents three down-to earth metaphors ("histories mean punch," "ghetto prisans," and "societies ghetto mentality") and other unusual metaphors, as in language being "molded" to fit a people's expressive needs and identity being "lost, stolen or astray," poetry being "a ticket to open protest." Max's use of affective kinship terms ("Black brothers and sisters") has been noted by Fordham and Ogbu as a strategy commonly used by African-Americans, but he takes the phrase to symbolic lengths when he follows it with "the aid of our white brothers and [sisters]." But most striking of all is his peroration, which so obviously draws on oratory. Although the solemnity of the sentiment is undercut by the choice of "Whack English," the impulse is pure, and the willingness to take a stand on difficult issues exemplary.

To see teachers' reactions, we can look to the readings of Max's essays by six of my colleagues. I instructed them to read the essays as if they were written in class by a freshman. Their comments were directed either to me, in which case they were not intended for Max's ears and thus may seem insensitive, or to Max as a student writer. The instructors who were asked to read this particular essay appeared to be aware of Max's potential and seem to be looking for ways to nurture it. Their responses are much to their credit in that they generally attempt to encourage Max's resourcefulness. While they realize that he is using diction that draws attention to itself, they do not let this fact interfere with their ability to judge the essay as a whole. A few of them are solely concerned with the essay's lack of unity or with its reliance on unsupported generalizations; the language itself does not seem to attract their notice. One comments on Max's style explicitly and positively: "Interesting reading due to style—variety of language rhythms; I like the use of figurative and vigorous language. . . . I am impressed with your 'voice' and sense of confidence." For this instructor, Max's style achieves its end; Max sounds impressive and intelligent (although the same instructor notes problems with unity, coherence, and development). Another reader similarly appreciates Max's style: "I do . . . like the 'oratory' style, especially in the conclusion. It seems especially significant if the writer is black, because it seems an affirmation of some aspects of black culture that black writers often avoid in academic discourse."

Yet this same instructor would be more cautious in advising Max about his writing. She does not want him to suffer from the ridicule she is afraid he may face. In the comment written for him she writes, "I like your concluding paragraph; it's very moving, though the 'Whack English' construction might make some readers laugh rather than think. You might not want to end such a powerful conclusion with such an unusual construction, especially if you want to be taken seriously." I believe this comment illustrates the sort of approach we should take with students like Max. We must try to divine his intentions, perhaps asking him to confirm our understanding, just as this instructor assumes that Max wants his readers to think. Then we must honestly explain how we think his words will affect an academic audience.

Fancy talk is likely to be another source of students' stereotypes for academic or educated language. As I have shown in Chapter 2, it is culturally associated with verbal skill and accorded both overt and covert prestige. Max's narrative displays a number of distinctive characteristics that may well be related to fancy talk. It is reproduced here exactly as it was written:

> It has once been said that children are the world's greatest resources. With this understanding, children desire a need to be active in showing the resources they possess. This activeness is not always granted to them, therefore children tend to get bored and restless. To combat boredom, children often find ways to get the attention of adults who seem too busy to allot the amount of time and attention desired from them. When I was a child I had ways to grasp enough lost attention to share with the entire nation of youth. I possessed an ability to create several different attention grabbers in which my mother and all other adults who came in contact with me would never forget.
>
> First of all my mother was always busy during my childhood. She contributed her lack of energy or time to her exhausting job hours. My mother worked an 11 o'clock A.M. to 7 o'clock A.M. shift which left her in a deep sleep during the times I was most alert. This cre-

ated a huge problem because I could not keep her awake and she could not keep me asleep.

During my boyish youth, I became very acrobatic. There was nothing I could not leap over or jump on. This tactic seemed to be most rewarding, for attention was spelled all over my backside. As soon as my mother would shut her eyes to sleep, I would leap onto her bed and perform my acrobatic feats. These things always gained for me an over abundance of attention because everyone feared I could jump onto and ruin something of value to them. Therefore, no one ever slept when I was awake. I was very brainy, wasn't I? Because of my keen creativity and untireing curiosity a careful eye was placed upon me where ever I ventured.

As my acrobatic feats wore off, I began to get into other mischieveus things. I began to cook at the age of three. I cooked an array of items which made me never feel neglected, for the fire department, neihbors and relatives flocked from all over to witness the phenomenon of my accomplishments. I cooked ice cream and fried cake, refried leftovers and became very familiar with all cooking utensils: However, this type of attention still did not satisfy me.

Continuing in my childhood growth, I began to want friends who would accompany me in my duty as a kid to communicate with adults. To my dismay, none would assist me in placing screwdrivers in my mothers nose in order to gain her assistence in checking my underpants for cleanlyness. Since no one else would help me, I created my own friend, Piggy, through whom all my actions were blamed. What ever mischive was discovered, Piggy was the cause. Piggy and I roamed the house doing all types of neat things. We locked my mother out of the house upon several occasions, hid keys, at sweats before dinner together, and complained to be lonely when we ran out of things to do. We helped each other gain enough attention to open an attention for sale shop.

Finally, all of my needs of attention were quenched when I became old enough to be sent away from home. My mother found every possible activity, sport, and summer camp to send me to in order to free herself of my energetic mode. All of a sudden I had no time to rest between rehersals here, and practises there. It turned out that all of my efforts to gain attention back fired and to this day I am paying for it.

Since Max's essay emphasizes narrative, it is conceivable that he could be praised for its voice. Though his diction may be seen as odd ("needs were quenched") and excessive ("every possible activity, sport, and summer camp"), his personality certainly comes through strongly and energetically, which is in keeping with his portrayal of himself as a child. In fact, the reaction of instructors to this narrative is generally positive in this regard. One reader comments that the piece has "a great deal of honesty and personality"; he also notes its "vigorous and varied diction." Another "enjoy[s] some of Max's word choices and descriptions."

Diction is occasionally misused, as if Max were unfamiliar with the words' connotations, although I surmise this is at least partly the result of creative license and attention to sound over sense, as we see with fancy talk (Dillard 247). As with the rhetorical strategies of copiousness and amplification, synonyms or redundant phrases are frequently piled together, as in Max's "boyish youth," or "time and attention" or "every possible activity, sport, and summer camp." The essay is marvelous in many ways, for example when it employs concrete, familiar language appropriate to a personal story. However, this rather ordinary concreteness is offset by places where the diction swells to grandiose proportions, for example, "Continuing in my childhood growth, I began to want friends who would accompany me in my duty as a kid to communicate with adults. To my dismay, none would assist me in placing screwdrivers in my mothers nose in order to gain her assistence in checking my underpants for cleanlyness." I can see a possible ironic reading here, as Max tries to comment indirectly upon his serious yet childlike attempts to get attention.

While many academics would probably find Max's writing style excessive, we should not assume that all would immediately censure it. Judgments of style are to a large extent subjective and culturally conditioned. In fact, many good teachers will recognize that Max's style shows signs of effort and growth. He actually may be praised for his innovative use of diction, for the risks he takes, or for the more "mature" sound of his prose. Much of the reaction will depend upon the teacher-reader's understanding of the student-writer's task. She will reward risk-taking behavior if she is aware, as Bartholomae is, that students imitating the rhythms and projects of academic discourse may at times miss the mark ("Inventing" 158).

One reader comments on Max's effective "figurative and vigorous language," and rates his persuasive essay high on voice and use of language (although he remarks negatively on nonconformity to the "conventions of Standard Written English"). As far as this teacher is concerned, Max radiates confidence. Yet another reader believes that Max is not really engaged in the topic of this essay (Black English), that he uses "pseudo-inflammatory rhetoric" to cover his lack of anything substantial to say: "There's no real energy there," this teacher comments. Had I not known firsthand of Max's deep interest in Black English, I might have drawn the same conclusion. The issue, then, is one of learning to build a solid academic argument as opposed to projecting insincerity.

The other informants who wrote for this study drew much less than Max on fancy talk. However, it does appear the writing of all four males is influenced by it as well as by traditions of public oratory, probably preaching. Polo, for example, begins his narrative with humorous hyperbole, by mixing the dramatic and the academic (in this case, the enumeration of points to be discussed):

> Ah, the fated seat belt. Yes, I happen to have a interesting story to tell concerning myself and the seat belt. First, I'll begin with my opinion on wearing seat belts, then I'll tell my story, and finally I'll conclude with how I feel about the seat belt law.

He goes on to tell a very short story about a car accident. He obviously did not have enough time to do a good job on this essay, but the flair of the opening is worth noting.

A similar use of diction is evident in Spike's essay on recruitment and retention of African-Americans at the university:

> Since the 1960's Black's have made important steps at achieving racial equality. Unfortunately, the University of Texas has not been a progenitor of racial equality and for this and several other reasons UT Austin this university has had difficulty at recruiting large numbers of Black students.

The essay goes on for two more paragraphs but is not finished. Other notable uses of diction include "these Black students are the majority in their microgaism of society" (an attempt, of course, at "microcosm"); "This one factor often makes it difficult to merge into the larger sector of white students"; and "This just means that a student takes in total aspect of college, past and present, into consideration when chosing a university." These sentences reach for elevated concepts while struggling with the vocabulary of academic discourse.

Thomas' prose also shows a subtle hint of the fancy talk tradition, particularly in his choice of "intellectual" or "big" words:

> Frequently, many of us have had what is termed "close calls," often viewing the event as simply a minor irritation. On reflection, those affected often shiver with apprehension when we realize how very close that particular event came to rendering as one last breath. I have had one such occurrence which, when recalled inflicts chills that force my body to consciously shiver.
>
> The date was July 15, 1983. I was on my way to a benefit for the Castle Hills Baptist Church. In it I played percussion for the twelve Days of Christmas. On the highway (410 west), my sister and I were en route to the church when a grey audi opted to break! On the highway! Well, we breaked the car locked its wheels and proceeded to turn horizontal to oncoming traffic. It was then that I saw the truck that would be my demise. It was barreling toward the disabled car at at least seventy miles per hour. It struck us. And then I knew nothing.
>
> A shaking hand on my shoulder awakened me. My sister screamed in tears to wake up. Blood dripped from my forehead as I emerged from the mangled vehicle. I was alive, unnerved but alive.

Thomas seems to have selected his words with care. For example, his use of "shiver" ("those affected often shiver with apprehension") is evidently a second choice; he has crossed out "wince" and written "shiver" above it. And he has changed from "impulses" to "chills" ("inflicts chills"). Besides some minor corrections and a tense change, these are the only revisions Thomas makes on this draft. (I do not know whether he made an earlier draft or outline.) At any rate, they show an attention to diction.

Thomas certainly has a flair for the dramatic, and this is partially illustrated by his abrupt ending. When he told me the story (after he had written it), I realized there was much more to it. He explained that he felt an abrupt end would be more intriguing to the reader. Again, his diction seems calculated to have an emotional effect on the reader, especially in the last paragraph, the "shaky hand," the sister screaming, blood dripping, and the mangled vehicle.

One expression ubiquitous to freshman English narratives is "proceeded to," usually mixed with informal language and often in stories about police or car accidents. It appears here like clockwork ("we breaked the car locked its wheels and proceeded to turn horizontal to oncoming traffic"). Its appearance supports the theory that Thomas is drawing on models of "official" language.

Thomas' essay on minority recruitment and retention at the

university is more conventional in tone and diction, as one would expect in a persuasive or expository piece. However, one paragraph in this short five-paragraph theme does call attention to itself by its unusual diction, and the conclusion is almost as stirring as Max's. The complete essay appears below:

> I agree that the University of Texas has tried to recruit more black students. This school, however, lacks a few area that vitally important to recruitment in general.
>
> To begin with, UT-Austin is situated in a state where grant and fellowships are based upon the sell of oil. The decline in the purchase of various oil reserves has made these stipends hard to come by, thus causing increased financial worries for the low-income student, to which blacks comprise the largest majority.
>
> Another weak point of our University is in its population. Due to its large size, it has been forced to become less personalized. Many would-be-longhorns, including blacks, are opting for more personalized schools like Baylor University, Rice and various out-of-state schools.
>
> But perhaps the biggest and insurmountable problem lies in the student body. Many of caucasian students at UT have been bred into the patterns of their forefathers of the 1800's. They view the attendance of black students as a necessary evil that may have to put up with, but do not have to mingle with. Thus there exists an undercurrent of racial hostilites which no one but the user can erode.
>
> I believe that this school of higher education is a great one. It has instituted such programs as SHARE and Preview to appeal to the young black student. But their efforts will continue to be for naught unless the students themselves decide to be, not niggers and honkeys, but simply, students with future goals to attain.

The fourth paragraph is the one that calls the most attention to itself. The metaphors are striking, yet they are not carefully worked out, as if the writer were speaking improvisationally. The breeding of racism, "mingling" with evil, and the erosion of racial hostilities are potentially powerful images. The "user" may be related to drug addiction or computers or simply evidence of grasping for an unavailable word like "perpetrator." The ending is certainly another attempt at drama on Thomas' part, and the final sentence is effective in its graphic use of "niggers and honkeys."

Spike's notion of narrative also pushes him to emphasize flair and drama in his language. His narrative is so concentrated on the element of surprise that it is cryptic. In our interview, conducted after he wrote the narrative below, he had to explain some of the missing details so that I could be sure I had followed the story correctly. He told me that his strategy was to heighten reader suspense:

> Life threatening incidents are always thought provoking and having a serious accident is no exception. An accident in which I was involved in had this same effect on me.
>
> It's a dark September nite (of course it is dark it is nite time!) and I am headed home. However this night I chose to use a less traveled route.
>
> The road was gutted with potholes and had turns that looked like a plate of spaghetti. The sound of the night wind rushing pass the car however, made the trip more than worth the little discomfort. The tunes emanated from the small door mounted speakers. "Don't you know that . . . Don't you know that . . . I bet a million dollar that you know that . . ." The beautiful ballad bellowed.
>
> It's a bright September morning, I lay nice a cozy, surrounded by the familiar objects in my room. However something was different. There was lots of chattery outside my door. "Who the hell wakes up this early? . . ." I looked outside the window. In a driveway sat a burned and contorted piece of metal. I went back to bed. "My car!" I screamed. An hour later, again I woke, but this time with a startling revelation, "What if the car would have hit me here? (head-on) What if . . . "

Spike uses a few devices besides fancy diction (like "road stuffed with potholes," "tunes emanated," and "burned and contorted piece of metal") to achieve dramatic effects. For example, he uses ellipses to indicate dramatic pauses as well as lapses in time, and alliteration ("beautiful ballad bellowed"), perhaps to recreate his sense of well-being before the accident. Most notable is the overall parallel structure of the essay, highlighting the contrasts between danger and safety: the "dark September nite" versus the "bright September morning" and the safe feeling in bed versus the wrecked car outside the window.

Of course, in Spike's case as in the others, this is a response to the demands of freshman English teachers—that narrative be exciting, vivid, personal, concrete. But when Spike and his peers in this study rise to the demand, they probably draw on fancy talk and preaching (and perhaps storytelling) as a resource that has been nurtured in their culture. All of these young men have a decided sense of style and are very aware that their words can be used affectively as means to persuasion. They seem to enjoy verbal play and performance, to relish word choice. They have an adventurous attitude toward words, and this is their strongest asset as writers.

Hedging Your Bets: Fancy Talk as a Rhetorical Strategy

Fancy talk and other forms of "high" style can be useful to BEV speakers in many contexts. For example, here is an excerpt from a conversation between Max and Polo concerning language attitudes, a topic both take seriously:

> It was, uh, brought to my attention that Black English per se could be a form to separate, of keeping blacks separated from, uh, the white society, uh, in a sense of secluding our conversations from, uh [*laughs*] other people.

There is a strange mixture of the playful and the serious here; Max is dead serious about the subject, yet he laughs in places. And there is also a mixture of the formal and the informal: The passive voice and the Latin per se construct an ethos that is somewhat detached, able to back off at any moment and break into a joke on the one hand, or on the other to turn to the serious issues that underlie the topic. Even though he is being serious and, presumably, using big words to signify his knowledge, he is careful in this passage not to commit with his voice. Laughter occurs in many of the instances where I find fancy or elevated language in his ordinary discourse. There is perhaps a guardedness, protection from the judgment of the white teacher/researcher, which comes, I believe, from a culturally conditioned caution.

Besides the serious sacred strain in artful African-American language, there is the playful secular strain. Behind both lies the model of life as conflict that Abrahams claims influences African-American folklore (*Positively Black* 30-31). When conflict is always possible, the prudent man, the survivor, the man-of-words, keeps his options open. In other words, fancy talk helps Max successfully construct an impressive ethos. He can hedge his bets so as to appear witty and humorous or intelligent and serious, as the situation and his interlocutor demand. Indirection of this sort (or "purposeful ambiguity," according to Mitchell-Kernan, *Language Behavior* 103) is not uncommon in BEV, as, for example, in signifying. Kochman reminds us that the intent of such indirection is "to place the receiver in the socially accountable position" ("Strategic Ambiguity" 153). As Kochman makes clear, in such instances, the receiver determines the direction the interaction will take. We can see this phenomenon in Max's interviews with his peers.

In an interview with Spike, Max uses the rather impressive-sounding big word *transcended*. A big word appearing as Max introduces a new topic becomes a contextualization cue for Spike that a performance, playful or serious, is offered. They are discussing the transition from summer school to the regular fall semester:

Max: Um, so, how has the transition transcended (*laughs*) from the summer to the fall?

Spike: What transition? It's just like whoosh; it's like meshed all together (*laughs*), you know? What summer? What fall? (*laughs*)

Spike's answer takes up the playful cue in Max's voice. His delight in "Whoosh" echoes Max's alliterative experiment with "transition transcended." He might instead have treated the subject seriously. Max lets Spike pick the direction of the talk. Max can be noncommittal. Spike might find a serious treatment of this subject inappropriate, so Max will not risk offering one. The big word *transcend* functions as a cue which signals that Max is performing and that Spike should respond to his performance by indicating what direction he wants the conversation to go, serious or playful. Because Spike and Max have known each other since the sixth grade, we expect informal discourse in this situation. Consequently, we might suppose that the only correct interpretation of this text is that it is humorous and light. But, because they are being taped and because Max sees himself as a research assistant collecting data on Black English, there is a serious element to the whole conversation we cannot ignore. Perhaps Max's perception of himself as interviewer whose job it is to elicit discourse also explains why he allows Spike to direct the conversation.

Max's use of fancy talk to hedge his bets also comes out in his conversation with Thomas, who, because of his negative attitudes toward BEV, might arouse more caution in Max. In the beginning of the interview, Thomas does use some BEV in informal chatting about "babes" (see Chapter 1). After this informal discussion, Max and Thomas get serious, and suddenly fancy talk, initiated by Max, occurs (at the word "intertwine"):

Max: Talk to me about your ideas on the frat.
Thomas: On, like A Fie?
Max: A Fie, New Pie, Omega.
Thomas: You mean, you mean the black frats? Or, you know . . .
Max: The black frats. And your ideas of what you want to do to, you know, intertwine frats together in the Greek system.
Thomas: Well, I'd like to try before I graduate to infiltrate, as it were, infiltrate the A Fie's system, you know, and work my way on up, you know, and, and then try and get them, . . . to just, just get off the high horses, you know, and kind of just mingle with the, with one of the white frats, but, . . . just to do something together instead of, you know, doing all, . . . this stuff by themselves. You know, when they're sitting around, you know, they're just chilling out by themselves. You know, when they go out and do something like babes and all that kind of stuff they're by themselves. Again, everything we do is black and everything they do is white. And there's got to be a happy medium somewhere.

Thomas continues at length to discuss his ideas. As he begins this passage phrases like "infiltrate, as it were" show his intention to sound important and intellectual. I contend that he would not identify this as anything but SAE himself, but that it is in fact also influenced by fancy talk. It has a different quality from other passages where he discusses a serious subject. Why it occurs here and not elsewhere is inexplicable, but it may have something to do with the tone of Max's question, which itself has the air of fancy talk ("intertwine frats together"). At any rate, it appears that Thomas has picked up on Max's serious intent, cued by his phrase "intertwine frats together."

Another case of fancy talk occurs at the beginning of Max's interview with me, although here it seems less a hedge and more a way to help us both relax. Asked if he will enjoy spring break and his mother's cooking, he replies with a comment on his dorm's (Jester) food: "All Jester food that I've consumed will be ejaculated from my system." Both of us laugh at his word choices. Max rarely uses fancy talk in his interview with me, although his speech is usually formal and serious and generally standard in style and diction. He has a finely tuned sense of appropriateness.

His use of fancy talk in this context is entirely appropriate and effective. Used judiciously, for example to be humorous, his artistry gains my good will.

I hear a commitment to the secular strain of fancy talk, in its playful aspect, when Max begins and closes interviews of his peers with a game in which he portrays a radio announcer or, perhaps, a talk show host. He plays this role in all cases except the opening of his interview with Thomas. He told me later he had done so to put his informants at ease, and I believe his strategy was successful. By giving them a role to play, he allows them to participate in his performance. Since they are aware that I would eventually listen to their taped conversations, they need protection, at least until they can relax. The examples that follow are full of play, verbal flourishes and big words for the sake of comedy. They are performed in a markedly different tone of voice, a low, slow delivery that mimics a show business personality. First, notice how he closes his interview with Thomas:

Max: (*shouts*) So this culminates another interview with Max Southerland, live, here at The University of Texas in Austin. With, um, the Thomas Penn, none other than the predominant international law progressive (*tsk*) student here at the, uh, University Undergraduate School of, uh, Business, and he (*tsk*) has exceptionally accepted the, um, aura in which (*laughs*) he has been forced into. Therefore his forth wherein he does plan to (*tsk*) initiate some affirmative action to where he will, uh, change the system at hand and, uh, presumably, produce a more comfortable environment for all races. (*almost whispers*) Thank you. And have a good day. (*snaps his fingers*)

In this case, fancy talk creates humor and puts the audience, not only the interviewee but the silent researcher who will listen to and report on the conversation, at ease. Max's ethos is positive. He uses the discourse to show his cleverness and creativity and to control the situation, defusing any tension. The appearance of Max as a "personality" at both the beginning and end of the tape suggests that he is bracketing the whole interview with an implication to take it seriously or not.

Max uses the same device of mimicry when he interviews Spike. On the day one tape was made, I met Max and Spike in my office and had a short conversation with them about what English classes they might want to take next. I turned the recorder on as I left them alone. The tape starts with some indecipherable whispering, although the phrase "She's gone" comes through clearly. Then, after some conversation about how good it is to get inside information on which classes to take, Max takes control and starts the interview proper. The quality of his voice noticeably changes, as it deepens and slows:

Max: So, uh, as (*tsk*) we're here live with Spike Jones here at The University of Texas at Austin.
Spike: Oh! I was going to ask you! George Smith. He goes here, right? Is he in the choir cause I heard
Max: He was there, he was at the
Spike: I got to see him. I still want to see him. (*laughs*)
Max: I wish. Hilarious. You know, I, we were walking by, (*falsetto*) "Hey, how's it going?" Well, he, you know, doesn't know you till you go up to him, (*more quietly*) "What's happening?"

Although Spike has ignored Max's offer to enter into the game and take on the interviewee personality, he does relax and begin to discuss a mutual friend, George, whom they both go on to mark. Mitchell-Kernan describes *marking* as a form of indirection in which one comments on another's behavior or language by mimicking their direct words (*Language Behavior* 137). Spike has picked up on the playful strain in Max's line and been diverted from the distraction of my presence. Max, in his role as research assistant, constructs a bridge of fantasy that allows Spike to forget the recorder. If Spike had not interrupted, Max could have continued the interview with a serious question.

Max also ends his interview with Spike using this device; it is another particularly jovial and amusing performance. We can almost picture him in a glass booth with a mike before him and his distinguished guest at his side:

Max: Well, ladies and gentlemen, this concludes the forum on, uh, Meet the Press here (*Spike laughs*) at The University of Texas at Austin, with the, uh, now aspiring Spike Jones, very well known, uh, (*Spike laughs*) businessman (*Spike laughs*) soon to be corporate general (*Spike laughs*) of affairs in the, uh, (*tsk*), not civilian but military world (*Spike laughs*) and, uh, we have culminated and completed yet another interview with none other than Max Southerland live at The University of Texas at Austin here in Parlin one oh nine. (*Spike laughs*) Thank you for your support.

Notice how long the first sentence is and how Max himself did not even pause in his performance to laugh. It is a smooth and masterful performance indeed.

In his interview with Polo, Max uses the same sort of style to open, but unlike Spike, Polo decides to play the offered part:

Max: Live from, uh, room one twenty five, Parlin, I'm here with Sir Polo Smith, master of the, uh, [tsk] once engineering now pre-law world (*Polo laughs*). He's a scholarly individual whom, uh, I feel will benefit us very greatly in his remarks and worldly comments. (*more quietly*) So, Mr. Smith, uh, nice to have you with us today. (*Polo laughs*) Tell me, uh, (*back to louder voice volume*) what has your experience been in the transition from summer school to the fall?

Polo: Well, I feel for one that, as a participant in the summer school, in such a rig-, rigorous schedule to begin with that I was greatly benefited from the fact that I had to do the work and my peers, I should say my peers and colleagues, we were all in the same, in the same boat per se. We were all hard workers and we had intelligence. And we all each study hard each and every night so having that good environment surrounding helped me to keep, keep up with my work.

It is clear from Polo's use of words like "rigorous," "peers," "colleagues," "per se," and "environment" (followed immediately by its synonym "surrounding[s]") that he is laying it on thick. It is unlike his conversations with me, where, although he may use big words, he uses them in moderation. Here, as even the quality of his voice makes evident, he is picking up on Max's game. The conversation continues with Max keeping up the performance. Fancy talk marks the dialogue:

Max: OK. Do you feel that, uh, there was a very broad transition from the summer to the fall? And could you elaborate on that?

Polo: Well as far as the transition it wasn't as, um, such a broad transition for me personally because I had the experiences from the summer. . . . But I also have found that in the fall I have more time; therefore, it's easier to procrastinate and put work aside.

The conversation continues as Polo elaborates a bit, then Max brings up the topic of basketball, and suddenly fancy talk fades out as the tone becomes comfortably informal.

However, Polo goes back to fancy talk later in the interview, almost as if he had decided to play the interview game again, and he does so in response to Max's reading from the list of possible questions I had given him:

Max: (*reading*) Have you met anyone here who really made a good or bad impression on you? (*laughs loudly*)
Polo: (*laughs*) On a good note, (*laughs*) I must say that I've been fortunate to meet Mr. Max Southerland, (*laughs*) a close friend.
Max: Yes, elaborate on that? Yeah?
Polo: (*imitating a popular comedian*) That's the ticket (*laughs*).
Max: Let's talk about the frats. Um (*laughs*).

Max takes up the game for a minute, dismisses the question about meeting people, probably because it is not his and is irrelevant to him, and goes on to a question he knows will get a more serious and lengthy response. At his mention of frats, the conversation does get serious again, for Polo has quite a bit to say on the subject. Evidently, when Max reads from the list he reminds Polo of their status as research informants and of the covert audience witnessing their performance.

Despite the obvious pleasure they derive from this conversation, it has a serious side: both Max and Polo make important points about fulfilling the role of good student. Polo means what he says. He and his friends did work hard in summer school and were better prepared for the fall. Why should they couch their serious remarks in such playful tones? Probably because they are not alone. They know that I will listen to everything they say, and, this being the start of the interview, they are a bit nervous. Max may be nervous because this is his first interview. He is undoubtedly searching for a way to play the researcher role. As a matter of fact, the question about adjusting to school was one I had suggested he might use to get the conversation going. The use of fancy talk in this situation allows both Max and Polo to hedge their bets. If they sound a bit silly doing this interview stuff, it will be because they are goofing around. If I am inclined to take them seriously, however, the message is there.

In his interview with Thomas, Max made the following comment, which, seen in the context of ambiguity, illuminates somewhat the conclusion to his essay on Black English:

> What do you feel about the Black English issue itself? How will this documentary, this, I mean, uh, this conversation help to, uh, I don't know, kind of create a Whack English (*laughs*) White and Black . . .

It is, I think, significant that Max laughs at this point, but not because of a lack of seriousness. His discussions of language make it clear that he believes in the concept behind the term "Whack English." He is genuinely concerned about the labeling blacks suffer because of their language, and he is at the same time understanding of those who promote SAE. He wants to find a way to bridge their differences. So his seriousness cannot be called into question. Instead, his laugh functions to hedge his bets, to cue the listener that he or she may or may not take his comments seriously.

Talking Smart: Don't Mess With Me, I'm a Professional

Shanique, more than any of the others focused upon in this study, participates in the bad talk tradition—she is a smart talker, witty, irreverent, tough, and clever. Abrahams, basing his remarks on his own observations and on early sociological work by Ladner, mentions hers as one style used by females in interactions with males. As opposed to the naive type who is a good listener, easily impressed by a man's sweet talk, the sophisticate "asserts her self-sufficiency through an answering style, one which relies on joking smart talk to assert distance and make room for her own manipulation" ("Negotiating Respect" 73). However, Shanique does not limit her smart talk to interactions with males. In fact, my texts demonstrate that she talks smart not only in reporting her interactions with men but also in playful interactions with her female peers.

Using smart talking and the covert prestige of BEV strategically, Shanique talks about herself in ways that display her ethos as strong and effective; however, her writing, although it does convey something of her voice, especially in her letter, does not convey the same ethos. As her writing becomes progressively more formal, we lose sight of an independent and personal character behind it: the prose takes on an impersonal and uncommitted voice that recalls neither the objective professional nor the impassioned intellectual we might expect in academic discourse.

Following, as a brief example to which I will return later, is the opening to her most formal essay, the topic of which is hazing:

> In order to join a fraternity or sorority pledges are literally put through hell. Is it all worth it? When asked, most inactive members agree that it was probably not worth it and wouldn't go through with it again. However when asked if they tested pledges in a difficult manner, all agreed that they had, but couldn't give specific reasons as to why. So to become a member of such organizations one must be willing to put up with a lot of unnecessary anxiety, embarrassment and sometimes even physical as well as mental pain.

101

As I explained in Chapter 4, I asked six college instructors to read and comment on the essays I collected for this study. How do these instructors perceive Shanique's ethos as conveyed by this essay? Certainly neither impassioned nor committed. One comments that Shanique seems to lack commitment to the topic and that she does not make her stand clear because she has not given the topic "much thought." Another writes:

> It's quite clear that Shanique doesn't have a complete enough under-standing of UT sorority/fraternity pledging and hazing activities, as she states [in the conclusion]. . . . And because these activities are of no great concern to her, she's not been forced (before the writing of this essay) to form an opinion of the subject.

Yet Shanique's interview with me, conducted before she wrote the essay, shows that she has indeed given the topics a great deal of thought and knows exactly where she stands.

For contrast to the essay opening, a brief section from her interview with me is transcribed below. (I return to it at the end of this chapter.) Unfortunately, a transcription cannot really capture the intonation, facial expressions, and gestures that contribute to her ethos in spoken discourse.

> Personally, I'm against it [hazing] because some people are kind of weak, especially mental hazing because I think, okay, that like, forc-ing somebody to drink, I think they must kind of sort of want to drink, too because ya, after a while you say "I can't take it anymore" and just take a stand and, I mean, . . . why would you want to be a part of a group of people who won't let you think on your own? But mental hazing, I think that's, that's kind of bad . . . but, um, I think it's, I mean, for people to do that, they shouldn't want to torture peo-ple like that. 'Cause messing with somebody's mind is serious, and I . . . I don't think it's right to do something like that, and I think they should be prosecuted. If they can be proven to do it.

Unimpassioned? Uncommitted? Shanique falters and repeats herself, a natural result of trying to collect thoughts as one speaks, but she adds details like quotes and personal experi-ence that show she really has thought about and cares about the issue. In fact, she comes out strongly against hazing. At the end of this chapter, I present the essay in full along with a larger portion of the interview for more detailed analysis. It will be even more obvious in the face of the fuller evidence that Shanique's ethos in written discourse does not convey her true stance on this issue. For now, I simply wish to contrast the ethos she constructs in speaking and in writing.

Generally, instructors were not impressed with this essay, and I would agree with their assessments. As the excerpt from Shanique's interview with me shows, she could have written a much better essay. Granted, she may not have felt the need to perform well for an ungraded essay. In contrast to Max, who spent the full seventy-five minutes writing, and who not only used a dictionary but asked me about the grammar of one sentence, Shanique wrote in about forty-five minutes and showed no further evidence of being engaged in the task. That is not to say that she was not—only that she did not demonstrate any concrete behavior to contradict the statement that her writing is superficial and detached. Certainly Shanique did show concern for doing well as an interviewer, and she did some limited revision of this essay, as indicated by cross outs. In addition, she showed a genuine interest in the topic of hazing not only in her interviews with me but also in other interviews. Furthermore, she had two topics to choose from for her expository essay, hazing and minority recruitment and retention at the university—both of which she had discussed in her interview—and she selected hazing.

I believe that Shanique's disengaged and apparently unconcerned ethos is not the result of her lack of commitment to the topic of hazing but instead is indicative of a weakening of her ethos as she shifts from the informal spoken to the formal (and academic) written mode. More specifically, her ethos is to a large degree dependent on cues such as intonation, gesture, and facial expression which are not available to her as a writer. Even more to Shanique's disadvantage, however, is that her ability to enhance her ethos by switching into BEV and drawing on smart talk is impaired. As a model student, she is well aware that BEV is prohibited in academic prose. Shanique does not, as Max does, compensate well for this loss or find written strategies to replace the vocal.

Shanique as Smart Talker

The smart talking ethos Shanique constructs in her spoken discourse tells us much of what we need to know about what happens when she shifts to writing. To understand better that ethos, we should review what facts we know about her and then consider her self-descriptive statements.

As we earlier learned, Shanique, seventeen at the time of the study, had earned a grade of *B* in my freshman English class the summer before. She seemed especially bright and attentive, and was always willing to participate in class. Shanique is from Jacksonville, a small town in northeast Texas. A year after the study, she announced plans to major in pharmacy or computer science, and two years later she was indeed a computer science major but planning to switch to liberal arts, English, or advertising. By the time she graduated, she was applying to graduate business schools. Her most recent position has been as an assistant editor for a trade publication.

The ethos Shanique constructs is in many ways conventionally acceptable to a mainstream audience. She values strength, independence, and power, including the symbols of power, such as the Cadillac for her mother and the Jaguar for herself she dreams of buying, or the medical degree she plans on getting. It would be difficult not to admire her or to believe that she is not admired by others for her character, as some of her stories claim. In some ways, her image conforms well to what society at large expects of an educated woman: well-dressed and groomed, secure in her body image, sure of who she is and what she wants, independent, and bent on self-improvement, especially economic and educational self-improvement. Shanique comments that she does not waste time and is a serious student who puts her homework and classes before parties and dating. She tells Laurie, "I plan for the future," and this statement is confirmed by consistent references to her plans for medical school.

Nor does she accept a subservient role in relation to men. Sweet talkers coming on to Shanique with smooth lines and the intention to deceive will be sure to fail miserably, as did the male friend who told her "I know exactly what you need." As Shanique tells the story to Laurie, she answered, "You don't know what I need. Don't nobody in this school know what I [*I* is emphasized] need, cause Shanique is the only person know what Shanique needs, all right." With characteristic humor, Shanique also tells Laurie: "Some guys'll say 'If you, if you go out with me, you gonna have to put out.' I say, 'If we go out in my car, I'm sure gonna put out. I put you right out of the car!'"

Shanique tells Dinese that she plans to have her own bank account and credit cards even after she marries. And she will always work. When she and Dinese discuss marriage and its possible effect on their careers, she says:

Shanique: I couldn't sit at home. I'd go crazy, cause I, I, uh, hum, I have to get out and exert myself.
Dinese: I have to feel like, I have to use this education that I've been . . .
Shanique: Yeah.
Dinese: . . . struggling to get.
Shanique: Yeah, 'cause like my grandmama always say, "No matter what you do, get your education, 'cause can't nobody take that away from you unless they take your brain." I said, "Well, shoot. Sometimes I wonder if my brain's going to last." (*Dinese laughs*)

Shanique's marking of her grandmother, in which she imitates her voice as well as directly "quotes" her, is characteristic of her lively style of speaking; she often uses narrative and marking to make her points. Her storytelling skills are excellent, and she is a joker and inveterate talker. In fact, she usually talks more than her interviewees, and occasionally interrupts them. However, Shanique can also be an attentive and sympathetic listener.

In spite of this conventional side, Shanique also presents an unconventional ethos, especially for a woman. From the perspective of the white, mainstream academic, her brand of toughness is suspect. For it, she draws on African-American culture. This side of Shanique values being tough, cool, and unwilling to countenance disrespect; in short, she is *mean*. Along with the mean Shanique comes a different kind of intelligence, the kind she celebrates in many of her narratives, that makes it possible for her to "pull one over" on the grownups by making them think she is an angel when she is really always into mischief. This Shanique is an "instigator," as she proclaims in her letter ("And you know me. I just sit back and instigate.") and her spoken narrative ("I am the main instigator."), not unlike the signifying monkey of African-American folklore, who gets others to fight while he sits back and enjoys the show. As Abrahams and Labov have demonstrated, BEV is often associated with exactly this sort of image. It is one of the images that promotes the covert prestige of the dialect.

As Shanique tells it, her two-year-old cousin Ashley serves as a miniature mirror version of this side of Shanique's character;

relatives are quick to point out the similarities between them. In telling me about Ashley, Shanique, obviously proud, explains:

> She [Ashley] kind of mean, too. Everybody say she takes after, they say she acts the same way I acted when I was little, 'cause she always get books and just be reading stuff and always writing on stuff and so hyperactive.

The mirror image of Shanique is a positive one from her perspective: a scholar on the move, always having to "exert" herself, and putting up with no disrespect.

Ashley and Shanique are both called *mean* by Shanique's mother:

> My Mom say, "I hope she don't be like you, Shanique, cause she's mean." But, okay, I said, "Hey, she'd be a great little girl, then." 'Cause she' got a good model.

Shanique's ethos is so mean, in fact, that her uncle, an Army recruiter, tries to convince her to sign up because she would make a great drill sergeant with her loud voice that carries an air of authority: She reports him as saying to her, "People listen to you. They have no choice." But Shanique is too smart to be tricked by a recruiter, even if he is her uncle. When he tries to convince her to sign up she says to him (or so she tells Dinese), "Wait. I'm your niece. Tell me the truth."

Shanique does not intend her listeners to take her meanness entirely seriously. Instead, it is calculated to bring her respect for her strength and intelligence. For example, she brags to Laurie that she beat up one young man: "Oh, girl, the other night did I tell you I beat him up? . . . And then I asked him to let me get into the Kappa dance for free." But, of course, as she quickly admits, she did not really beat him up. The whole story comes out as she and Laurie talk. It turns out he had been bothering her and challenging her, and so her account of the incident is colored by bravado:

> 'Cause he kept, he kept punching on me, I say, "Stop, little boy!" 'Cause he insisted he's taller than me. Laurie, I be standing up, he come up to me, looking up at me, "Who's the tallest?" (*Laurie laughs*) I'm going, "Boy, I spit in your eye."

She tells Divinity a similar story about almost beating up a sorority girl:

Shanique: I started to hit her on top a the head. (*Divinity laughs*) She was going to walk on my toe. And look at me like it was my fault. I said, "Oh, you excuse me. Just don't try that no more."

Divinity: Where'd you see her at?

Shanique: We were walking, I was, I don't know where I was going, it was on, on that thing out there.

Divinity: Uh hum.

Shanique: West, East Mall.

Divinity: Uh hum.

Shanique: It was really crowded 'cause, it, people were voting or something. People was all shoving (*Divinity laughs*) and she stepped on my foot, and she looked at me, and . . .

Divinity: Oooo!

Shanique: I say, "Don't do that no mo'!" Made me mad.

Shanique's point is that she would not let a sorority girl intimidate her. Divinity's assorted "Uh hum's" and "Oooo's" show her approval and encourage Shanique to embellish her story.

Perhaps the most outstanding image Shanique presents is one of a woman who knows who she is and how to get what she wants. When one young man called her strange, a chameleon and a Gemini who changes all the time, she reports to Laurie that she told him: "I am not strange. I just know what I want." Likewise, in a discussion of snobbery in sororities, she tells Divinity: "I don't need to be no Delta. I know who I am." She tells me that she would like to join a sorority, but only so that she can "step in a Greek show," i.e., dance in one of the African-American sorority's staged events. In other words, she does not need a sorority to forge her identity, to wear their colors or to spend too much time at their parties: "You have to have time to go to classes and to the library. I can't think about going to parties and dressing in red and white and pink and green," she tells Divinity. On the other hand, she does not mind using sororities for whatever pleasure and benefit they can bring her. Sororities don't control Shanique. She controls them.

Covert Prestige of BEV

A notable aspect of Shanique's smart talking ethos is achieved by her quite extensive shifting into BEV in speech. As I explained in Chapter 1, style-shifts can be metaphorical, especially when unexpected in terms of the speech event type, and thus can display a speaker's or writer's attempts to construct an ethos. In Shanique's case it is not particularly remarkable that she uses BEV with Laurie, who also consistently uses it, nor with Divinity and Dinese, since though they seldom use it themselves they are able to do so. However, Shanique's seemingly unselfconscious use of BEV in interviews with me might be questioned, as might Laurie's. All the other informants, male and female, modify their speech almost entirely to SAE in this context.

One possible explanation is that Shanique and Laurie use BEV with me simply to be good informants, since they know I am interested in it. Another possibility is that their use is metaphorical: it shows their acceptance of me as a familiar. Yet they seem so unselfconscious in their speech that neither of these explanations seems adequate. Shanique's dialogue with Divinity about the article on BEV (Chapter 3) brings up another possibility, i.e., that she has little interest in the language issue. Since they are comfortable with BEV and able to use it to great effect in storytelling, and since they are comfortable with me, they naturally use BEV in talking to me. Perhaps they do not use the dialect metaphorically at all.

That is not to say that their use of BEV in such a situation does not affect their ethos. The question is really to what extent they consciously manipulate their use of the dialect in constructing an ethos. Certainly most bidialectals are somewhat aware of the attitudes of outsiders toward their nonstandard dialect. Shanique cannot be entirely unmindful of the covert audience, the readers of this study, who, she must know, might judge her on her speech. In keeping with the confident and proud ethos she constructs, she seems to use BEV in spite of their possible prejudices against it, almost as if to show them that an intelligent, independent, successful woman can speak BEV if she wants to with her head held high. In other words, she challenges the belief that BEV should not be used with a white instructor, at least when that instructor has indicated an acceptance of the dialect.

Furthermore, when Shanique is showing her mean side, she naturally turns to BEV as an integral part of the image she is projecting. Mean women just talk smart that way. She draws on BEV's covert prestige to construct the ethos of toughness, independence, and self-assured power often associated with BEV. Remember that not only African-Americans make such associations. The British pop singers studied by Trudgill provide an example of a group that found prestige, one worth imitating, in the pronunciation of African-Americans.

Under circumstances where Shanique is attending to her speech she may shift to BEV metaphorically, but her use of it is probably more often than not unconscious, a result of her feeling comfortable and unashamed and of BEV being her most informal and natural style. In one case, the use of *it is* for *there is*, she appears not to be conscious that *it is* is a BEV form. The following passage is interesting because we are discussing a more formal topic (sensationalism in news reporting), and it occurs at the beginning of our interview, before we have really relaxed and gotten used to the taping, a factor which would push us toward more formal and thus more careful discourse. Notice that in this excerpt about the movie *Angel Heart* Shanique consistently uses *it is* instead of *there is* as an expletive, a pattern I find throughout the spoken texts I have collected from her. The relevant features are highlighted:

> The theater was packed last night. . . . But it, I thought it was a pretty good movie cause it had all this, had all this voodoo and stuff, and I was just tripping. And it was, it was kind of scary. **It was** more violence than anything. **It wasn't** really any sex. **It was** really only one sex scene. . . . That was it. (*Shanique discusses the movie at length*) The movie was kind of confusing cause **it was** all this symbolism and stuff. . . . But it was, it was pretty good, if you weren't . . . expecting something else.

Elsewhere she uses a nonstandard verb form once ("people was going") and BEV slang once ("tripping"), supporting my contention that she is comfortable with BEV at this point in the conversation.

In speech, she uses *it is* as an expletive often. The list below gives a few more examples, besides those just quoted:

1. But it was a lot of controversy about his body and everything.
2. It was like twenty or thirty of us.
3. It was quite a few of us in Preview.
4. They say it's, it's just not enough black people on campus.
5. That's all it is to it.

In contrast, she uses *there is* in two sentences (in her letter) of the written texts, showing that she is not unaware of the form's use in SAE:

1. Well, I'll have fun cause there are going to be plenty of fellows . . .
2. Here there just ain't much except a few girls . . .

In a large number of spoken texts, I find no instances of *there is*, while in the small number of written texts, I find two instances. The implication is that Shanique unconsciously uses the expletive *it is* as a BEV feature which she has not extended to formal speech or to writing. In writing she uses the standard *there is* when an expletive is called for. Furthermore, she does not use the *it is* expletive in her writing. Thus, we can see in the case of expletives that it is not simply a matter of her using BEV unselfconsciously in speaking but also a matter of paying careful attention to her language that results in her using the appropriate style for academic writing.

The absence of BEV from Shanique's writing might be explained by the fact that she considers it inappropriate for college writing or formal discourse. Her schooling would have reinforced an exclusive association of the written code with SAE. Remember that I required her to use SAE in freshman English (except in dialogue) and certainly that has been her experience throughout her education. In other words, though she may feel BEV is appropriate in semi-formal spoken discourse and that it is nothing she should be ashamed of, she may feel just as strongly that only SAE is appropriate for writing. When she does use BEV in writing, it is self-consciously local dialect. For example, in her letter she writes "Well chil' how're thangs with you and yo man Ron?" And in the narrative she wrote for my class she used BEV in the dialogue of African-American characters, as in the following excerpt:

> "Skim," she called me that because I was so skinny; she said, "Skim, god still loves you, its just that he need Tony right now to help him in Heaven."
> "But what can Tony do, he only fourteen."

From Spoken to Written Discourse: Changing Ethos

The Shanique of the interviews is not the Shanique of the essays. Her mean ethos undergoes a rather marked change as her discourse becomes more formal and relies more heavily on SAE. The ethos she constructs in her interviews is tough and funny, intelligent, independent, and involved. Her letter retains many of these qualities. But her narrative and expository essays fall flat. Her ethos at its best is like that of any obedient student conforming to the dictates of an assignment. Except for occasional flashes of humor or insight, she seems uninvolved in her topics. And at worst, she seems not mean but cruel, not witty but silly. As we examine her discourse in more detail, the progression becomes apparent.

Of all the stories Shanique tells about herself, my favorite is the one she tells Dinese about her experience in high school working as a nurse's aide. It conveys her ethos so beautifully that, in spite of its length, I reproduce most of it here:

Shanique: I used to call the doctors by their first names and stuff.
Dinese: Um hum.
Shanique: I'd go, "Shit, when I become a doctor I want people to treat me like I'm a person, too." So I'd say, "How ya doing, Jerry?" and the nurses would like, look at me. And I'd look right back. I'd say, "He told me to call him by his first name. Gosh," I'd say. 'Cause they'd say, (*raises pitch and speaks more quickly and nasally*) "Dr. Newton, Dr. Newton." I'd say, "Hi, Jerry. How're ya doing?" . . . (*Tells about becoming closer to Dr. Newton and about Dr. Chang, who always spoke too loudly, and how she told him to lower his voice because, "You are in a hospital. People are trying to sleep, now."*) But our head surgeon, he was so cocky. And one day, he come, it was, all the nurses were gone from the station and me and my friend were sitting there talking. 'Cause we were doing our charts and stuff. He come through there and just fussing about something. I say, "Well, I'm not a nurse. I wouldn't know." (*imitating the doctor's voice in the dialogue that follows*) "Well, why you working here if you ain't a nurse?" I say "Because I'm working in my work study from school." He say, "Well, all these people don't know anything about anything." I say, "Well, hey, you don't have to get cocky with me. 'Cause if you a doctor, you should know everything. (*Dinese cheers*) I thought that's what doctors are supposed to do." And my fren' say, my friend . . .

Dinese: What'd he say?

Shanique: He just looked at me. And I say "And you gonna have to talk to me with respect." (*Dinese laughs*) 'Cause he say, "You been very disrespectful." I say, "To earn my respect," I say, "To get my respect, you have to earn it. And you have to give respect to get respect from this chick. That's all it is to it. I don't care who you are." And I says, "You ain't God. You don't get respect unless you earn it." 'Cause I was talking to him, he was just looking at me. He say, "I'll just talk to your supervisor." I say, "I don't care. I don't have to work, shoot. It's not like this is the only job on this planet." And then later, later, um, I was on the elevator, and he got on the elevator. And I wasn't going to say anything to him. He says, "Well, how you doing today?" And I just keep on looking straight ahead. He didn't call my name, so I figured he wasn't talking to me. And he say, "Excuse me, Miss Waters, how you doing today?" I say, "I'm doing just fine. Well, how are you?" He say, "I like your style, 'cause you have spunk. And don't let nobody get over on you." He said, "I tried my best to intimidate you, but it didn't work." I said, "Hey, you don't intimidate me." I go, "Shoot! You ain't nothing but a man. You can die just like anybody else will." And he say, "I like your style. I wish more people . . . were like you." I say, "Shoot!" I was scared. (*both laughing*) 'Cause I was sure he was going to go to the office and get me fired, and then I'd lose credit at school and stuff. Shit. I have to stand my ground.

As this story shows, Shanique may actually feel insecure and scared at times, but far be it from her to admit it or to back down when she has been insulted. Whether or not this story is true word for word is impossible to discern, but it does illustrate her attitude and her self-stylization as a smart-talking, mean woman.

What is fascinating about her ethos is the way she presents herself confronting danger. Her friend, she seems about to say, is ready to stop her from telling off the doctor, but she gives this rude and arrogant man his due and shows him that she is not to be trifled with. She is not like the obsequious nurses who are afraid to call the doctors by their first names or to tell them to lower their voices. The chief surgeon is not an easy conquest, however. He does not back down but threatens her job. When she next sees him (notice how she builds the tension by drawing out her account of the greeting), he not only treats her with respect but tells her he admires her spunk and her honesty.

Not only does Shanique thus present the narrative details with admirable precision, but she also tells the story in BEV, even though Dinese, to whom she tells it, has not spoken to her in BEV.

Dinese does speak informally, but the closest she comes to BEV is to use a few items of slang (as in "It just trips me out"). Clearly, then, Shanique is not using BEV simply in response to Dinese's conversational style. It seems to me that she tells this particular story in BEV because it suits the image she is building of herself. In short, in both the story itself and her manner of telling it she constructs the ethos she desires. Shanique's use of BEV is in some ways analogous to Max's use of fancy talk. In both cases, language is being used to construct an identity and a certain ethos, and in both cases hyperbole is a device that enhances the discourse. Max uses fancy talk to reproduce his stereotype of the way an intellectual writes or talks; Shanique uses BEV and narrative detail to reproduce her stereotype of the way a strong and independent woman (a mean woman) deals with a powerful man.

Another aspect to Shanique's ethos is the humorous, good-natured side that we might easily overlook by emphasizing meanness. She often sees the funny side of things. Probably one of the funniest stories she told me was about her niece Ashley:

> But she acts like a little old woman 'cause she stays with my grandmother during the day and she, my grandmother, my grandmother, she has a heart condition, but she won't slow down and she's always grunting. And my grandfather had lung cancer on one a his lungs and so he had a lung removed, so he's always panting for air. So they were, they both walk around grunting (*gasps*). And so Ashley, she be just (*gasps*). I was going, "God, that's a great imitation." You know, she's, (*gasps*) "Whew!" I say, "Are you tired?" "Uh uh." I say, "What you grunting for?" (*laughs*) "I'n 'ow." I guess she thinks that's the thing to do. I mean, she's, say, (*gasps*) and she's walking and talking and grunting. And I used to call her a little grunt.

Shanique frequently uses marking to create humorous effect. Her humor naturally enhances her ethos by securing the goodwill of her audience, that is, if they understand her humor. Because Shanique's stories are grounded in African-American folklore and culture and in stock characters such as the trickster and the bad man (discussed in Chapter 2), academics may easily misconstrue or overlook some of her tongue-in-cheek statements. This is especially likely to happen when she uses hyperbole and when she reports her "heroic" deeds.

Exuberance and humor characterize her letter (reproduced in Chapter 1). I imagine La Tonia enjoyed receiving it and laughed at the April Fool's joke. In keeping with the lighthearted tone, Shanique obviously intends this letter be read with her distinctive voice, the unique speaking voice she uses when she is being funny and informal. Her spelling of words like "chil'" and "yo" indicates that some thought went into the use of BEV. The apostrophe for the missing letter shows that she is deliberately using a nonstandard form. The same can be said of the spelling of "thangs," the regional "y'all," or "somethin'." She goes even further with her spelling of "do hurry" as "du hurra" and the phrase "Wished I could go." She seems to use dialect to increase the sense of familiarity between herself and La Tonia. Other very obviously oral features of this letter are her statement "oophs I'm repeating myself!" and her use of "Umph!" She underlines "serious" twice and "suitors" once to indicate that they should be stressed in reading. I can almost hear her chatter as I read this letter.

As Shanique moves from the informal letter to the semi-formal (or perhaps even formal) narrative, a decided change occurs in her ethos. She no longer seems willing or able to import the oral features that contribute so greatly to the exuberant ethos of her letter. Academic prose prohibits the use of mechanical emphasis like underlining, all capital letters, or exclamation points, and unorthodox spellings, drawings, and nonstandard grammar. Yet these provide much of Shanique's technique for imitating the ethos she constructs so easily in speech.

It is important to consider how the culture of the academy influences discourse, especially written discourse. Bartholomae proposes that students must appropriate a position in the discourse community, that they must "invent the university by assembling and mimicking its language" ("Inventing" 135). When Shanique sits down in a classroom with other informants to write a narrative, she takes on the role of a student approaching a school assignment. She is no longer having a friendly conversation or performing as an informant or researcher in a study. At least, these are no longer her primary roles; to the extent that she does see herself as an informant, I believe she conceives of her purpose as showing that as a BEV speaker she can be a good student. Comparison of the same story in a spoken and a written version illustrates the way context demands different rhetorical strategies and taxes Shanique's ability to meet the demands of written academic discourse.

Since she told me the story first, I will present her transcript first. Shanique told me this story in response to my question about a time she may have gotten in trouble or broken a rule. Her delivery is very fast, at times almost breathless:

Shanique: Well the worse thing my cousin and I did. My cousin, I have a cousin like two years younger than me, and everybody thought she was so bad 'cause she was extremely mean and stubborn, and she and I were feeding, my grandmother had chickens. And all my gran, all my cousins stayed at my grandma's house. All the time, practically, we practically lived there. And she and I, we got along great because she was stubborn and I always talked her into stuff, but she would always get into trouble. So, 'cause she would never say, "Well, Shanique told me." So she say "Yeah, I did it. What you gonna do about it?" So she would just take the blame. And she and I one day, we were feeding my grandmother's chickens. And we were teasing the chickens like, we had something, and I don't know what it was, but we, we put down that, we raise it up and we make, 'cause we want to see him jump. And the rooster pecked my cousin's, pecked my cousin's hand, so we said, "Yeah." And she cried, and afterwards we, we going, "Yeah, we gonna get that rooster. I ain't like that rooster anyways." And so, we were sitting up, sitting on the back porch thinking of something to do, and we was just thinking and so we, it was in July. It must have been close to July 'cause it was in the summer and we had firecrackers. So we decided to blow his beak off, so he couldn't peck anybody else. (*Valerie laughs*) So she, I held the chicken while she put the firecracker in his mouth and tied some string around it. We were very creative.

Valerie: (*laughing*) Oh God!

Shanique: And (*laughing*) and it was like one of those wild cats, one of them powerful little firecrackers.

Valerie: Uh huh.

Shanique: And, and the chicken was just a fighting, and so we lit it, and we blew his beak off.

Valerie: (*laughing*) Oh my God!

Shanique: And then we had to go ahead and kill the chicken cause it wouldn't stop bleeding, and then (*laughing*) we tried to bury it so we wouldn't get into trouble. (*Valerie laughs*) And then, and like, and so, that time we blamed it on the dog. We said, the dog, we said the dog got a hold of the chicken, and he was half dead so we went ahead and killed it. 'Cause my grandfather, we had chicken blood and we were, on our hands, we were like, my grandfather's like, "Who killed the chicken?" And we were like "Patches did it." He was the dog. "Patches killed that chicken." And poor Patches got beat. (*both laugh*) I say, hey, better the dog than us.

Valerie: (*laughing*) You got away with it, huh?

Shanique: Um hum. Yeah.

Valerie: How old were you then?

Shanique: Probably about seven or eight. (*Valerie laughs*) And then, one time my grandmother was keeping us, and my cousin and I just would not go to sleep, and we were just sitting on the floor laughing and stuff. And, uh, cause we, she, she make us, she put a quilt out on the floor and it was, we ca-, a pallet, and we get on the pallet and take our nap. And we were like in the back room, and we would not stop laughing, and my grandma said, "If I come back in there." If she had to come back in there she was going to, um, she was going to come in there on us. So we didn't want her to whip us or anything, so we lay on the floor and just, and we were just talking and stuff. We were stuffing the blanket in our mouth to keep her from laughing, from hearing us laughing, and we finally get kind of sleepy. And as soon as we get to sleep one of our neighbor's cats come along and it's "Meow, meow, meow" making all this noise meowing. I said, "I am so sick a this cat." And okay, my cousin say "Okay, let's get 'em then." So we got some, my grandfather's gasoline, where he had been mowing the yard. And we stroked the kitty cat with gas. "Here kitty, kitty, kitty." And we just stroked the ca- cat with (*Valerie laughs*) gasoline and stuff and set him on fire. And the cat went running. Haven't seen that cat since. And then (*laughing*) my grandmother's going . . .

Valerie: You were a terror.

Shanique: My grandmother's going, like, "I was in there taking a nap and all of a sudden I seen this big ball of fire come running yonder way. (*Both laughing.*) And, and she say, "Shanique and Mussie," my, we called her, my cousin, Mussie. I don't know why. Her name was Corsica, but people couldn't say that so we called her Mussie, and she say, "Shanique, Mussie in there just laughing and laughing." She say, "I wonder what they did to that cat." She say, "They always into something." And then she's going, "Well, Mussie anyway 'cause Shanique was the good one." (*Valerie laughs*) Oh I had them fooled. Still do. Everybody think that I am so angelic. I never do anything, and I am the main instigator. (*Valerie laughs.*) It was so funny. But . . .

Valerie: That's great.

Shanique: But it was a lot of (*laughs*) we did a lot of bad things when we were little. . . . One time when we left the chicken pen open, and she had a cow in there, too, and we shooed the cow, and we had a horse, and we got rid of it. We just let everything loose, and then we go, because my older cousins would have to go chase 'em down, and we wanted them to get outta, the chicken, she, they be watching the basketball game, and we wanted to watch cartoons. So we let all (*Valerie laughing*) the animals loose and they have to, "Chicken loose! Cow's gone! The horse is gone!" (*both laughing*) and they have to go running. We be in there watching TV like nothing (*Valerie laughs*) ever happen. I say, and then, my grandmother's going, "Who left the that chicken pen open?" "I'on 'ow." and whoever's, and I feel sorry for the one who went to collect the eggs 'cause he's the one that got in trouble. May not get any, he may not get a spanking but he got fussed at. And he nev-, but then he never have to go get the eggs again so that was the good part about it. (*Valerie laughs*) . . . And then I would go in the chicken's coop while the chicken was laying the egg. I would push that egg back up there in that chicken. (*Valerie laughs*) She say "I, I wonder what wrong with that hen?" 'Cause, (*screaming*) and I been trying to push that egg, I was trying to figure it out why she, and I said, "Hmm." It was interesting. I pushed that egg back up in there. And one time the chicken got after me. She was like (*laughs*) "I can't deal with it today, Shanique." (*Valerie laughing*) And that chicken, and that chicken must remember me 'cause every time I come to the chicken pen she either run or she come at me full force. But and (*laughing*) my grandmother and I was going, like I ask her all kinds of questions and my grand-, and like, I asked, "Where those eggs come from?" She say "Go see," and I went to see, so (*Valerie laughs*) I thought maybe if I pushed it back up in there she may, she, into the. 'Cause I thought, I asked her where do the babies come from. She say, "From the chicken." And she was laying the egg, and I thought if I pushed it back up there, then she'd have a chicken. (*laughs*) And so (*Valerie laughs*) I was trying a push the egg back up in there. I bet that chicken thought I was crazy.

Valerie: (*laughing*) You must have been quite a kid, I tell you.

Shanique: But I never got in trouble, though. That was the good part about it.

Valerie: Never got punished, really, that you can remember?

Shanique: Well, I got a few spankings, but most, a majority of the time I didn't. 'Cause I would alway-, and I, I had a lot of younger cousins, and I would always tell one of them to go do it, and they wouldn't say, "Shanique told me to!" They just sit up there and wonder why they were getting in trouble and why I never did. And they always looked up to me, and they always wanted to follow me. And I was trying to make 'em, figured if I made them get in trouble they wouldn't want to play with me and leave me alone.

Before we compare the written version of these stories, I want to point out that Shanique keeps returning to the theme of the false front. She is the devil everyone thinks is an angel. She mentions from the beginning that she and her cousin would get into mischief, dreamed up by Shanique, but that Mussie would always take the blame. Notice that Shanique portrays herself as an *insti-*

gator, showing a certain cleverness not unlike that claimed by the trickster figures of African-American folklore.

The stories fall into three narratives of parallel structures, each illustrating Shanique's character as an instigator who gets away with her misdeeds. The story about the rooster, which comes first, is introduced by her announcement of this theme. That story ends with the blame falling on the dog, and Shanique, hardly pausing to answer my question about her age at the time of these incidents, moves right to the story about the cat. The cat story is set up with a similar structure: evil cat keeps Shanique and Mussie awake, they take their revenge, and nobody gets in trouble (except the cat). There is a slight inconsistency here because Mussie shares the role of instigator. Shanique brings up the theme of her ability to deflect trouble to close the cat story, this time embellishing it a little more by mimicking her grandmother saying, "They always into something. Well, Mussie, anyway 'cause Shanique was the good one." Then she adds as an aside: "Oh I had them fooled. Still do. Everybody think that I am so angelic. I never do anything, and I am the main instigator."

She moves from my observation that a farm presents plenty of opportunities for children to get into trouble to another story, this one about letting the animals loose, that again illustrates her cunning and her ability to avoid punishment. I have deleted a story Shanique begins but abandons about mischief in the cow barn; she never gets far enough to make a point, but mention of the cow barn seems to remind her of the chicken coop and her curiosity about where chickens come from. After this diversion, the theme temporarily changes, though her character as a brave and curious child is still illustrated. She finally returns to her original theme at the end of this story by noting, "I bet that chicken thought I was crazy. But I never got in trouble, though." The cycle of narratives comes to an end with my question about her being punished. She describes how her younger cousins were easily manipulated into taking the blame for her, and then moves into stories about her cousins, especially her little cousin Ashley, who like Shanique is considered very bright and mean.

The almost shocking cruelty to the rooster and the cat are far less brutal when these stories are told than when they appear on paper. The way Shanique sets up the story, she and Mussie are taking sweet revenge on the rooster for hurting Mussie and on the cat for keeping them awake when their wakefulness could bring their grandmother's wrath upon them. The rooster especially seems to invite his fate: "So we decided to blow his beak off, so he couldn't peck anybody else." The girls take on almost folkloric stature, like those bad, bad men whom Abrahams describes in the toasts, Stackolee and Shine, the ones who have "a tombstone disposition and a graveyard mind" (Abrahams, *Positively Black* 45).[1] And they resemble the signifying monkey—who gets into mischief by teasing other animals and egging them on to fight, though he gets caught in the end—or the famous trickster Brer Rabbit. Shanique even embellishes her description of tying the firecracker in the poor rooster's mouth by adding, in a slower, more wry, tone, "We were very creative."

However, in the folklore tales, just because someone is spectacularly bad does not mean that what he does is condoned. Shanique shows how their deed of revenge goes from bad to worse, until "poor Patches" the dog is beat. On the other hand, as she puts it, "Hey, better the dog than us," showing sufficient remorse and yet still showing she avoids trouble by her wits. In the cat story, the grandmother is too amazed by seeing "this big ball of fire come running yonder way" to place any blame. Besides, she has no proof (the evidence has taken off in a ball of fire), but she definitely suspects Mussie. The story about letting the animals loose is also a sort of revenge tale, but this time she and Mussie are getting revenge on their older cousins for monopolizing the television set. The image of the two tiny girls, rather powerless, getting the better of their presumably male and certainly older cousins by virtue of their wits is irresistible. In this story, however, the revenge is not as cruel: The one left holding the bag may get a spanking at worst or be "fussed at" at best, but he will also be relieved of the chore of egg collecting.

Undoubtedly the assignment itself affects Shanique's approach to the written essay. Notice that it sounds very much like an assignment one would receive in a writing class, that it invites a thesis or generalization and specifies a general educated audience:

> Children often find ways to do what they want (have fun, satisfy curiosity) in spite of adult restrictions and threats of punishment. When you were a little girl, you managed to fool adults into thinking you were angelic, even though you often got into mischief or

instigated it. Write about some of your escapades on your grand-mother's farm.

A student who is able to play the academic game well will be aware that hints are being provided as to what will be a suitable thesis. Shanique takes the hint, but her first paragraph shows that she is so concerned with providing a thesis that she overdoes it. Shanique seems unable to focus on one particular theme. The introduction, where the thesis would be expected to appear, is overly long, giving the impression that she is groping for focus.

The invitation to "write about some of your escapades on your grandmother's farm" is vague enough to allow her to select among the incidents she mentioned in the interview or to provide others. Perhaps its very vagueness hinders her choice. At any rate, no one incident is discussed at length, and as a result, the sharp, rich narrative details, the quotations, the humor, and the exuberance are gone, and even the parts of the stories have changed, suggesting that the oral versions are embellished for the immediate listener or that the written version is truncated for economy and readability. Her cousin's more formal name, Corsica, is used instead of her nickname, Mussie. The rooster and the cat incident are revived, although the cat's fate is somewhat changed, and the comparison with Ashley, her young cousin, also remains.

Another expectation of a school essay is a clear structure, and Shanique meets that expectation with dismal results. The three paragraph format, a classic school essay pattern, allows for very little creative detail: the introduction makes some attempt at delimiting a theme, the second paragraph at illustrating it, and the third, at closing with a generalization about being older and wiser. The text is reproduced below:

> Are children smarter than adults? Some say no, but I think yes; or at least I think I was when I was a child. People say that children are allowed to get away with "murder" because they are so cute and adorable. In my case, this was not true, actually I was far from adorable, and definately not cute. I was a skinny little girl with big eyes and a deep voice. So I think it is a matter of whit that allowed me to have such a fun and worry-free childhood. Or it could be the fact that I was, and still am, my grandmothers favorite granddaughter. She says its because I was so sickly looking and she felt sorry for me; I say its because I was smart and knew how to win her heart! It was definately [*not* is omitted] because of cuteness, for my "cutest"

cousin who is some two years younger than I was marked as the most evil little child and was never allowed to get away with anything. Corsica, my cute little cousin, and I were, and still are the closest as two people can be. For our relatives this is hard to understand because we are so "opposite", I'm "angelic" and she's quite hellish, or so they think! Actually we are pretty much alike.

Upon remembering our childhood, it is funny to think of all the chaos that Corsica and I caused, and how she was usually blamed, but every once in a while, I did stand up, and took some blame, but not often. We really weren't that bad, the worse thing we did was kill a couple of chickens and a cat. To escape punishment for the death of my grandfathers chickens we used my uncle as a scapegoat or we blamed the family dog, Patches. As for the cat, no one like cats any ways, but my grandmother was not pleased with the fact that we decided to dispose of the cat in her wood-burning heater. Of course we pretended we didn't know what happened. Finally we admitted we'd done it, but only because the cat had scratched Corsica, really I scratched her. We needed an allabi and she could endure the pain. My grandmother got over it, but she couldn't believe that I let Corsica talk me into such a devious act. Actually I did the conniving.

Now that I'm almost an adult I tell my older relatives (grandma, grandpa, and mother) that Corsica and I both were the blame, but they insist that I'm just trying to cover for Corsica so they'll stop being so hard on her. Besides, they're solely concerned with a new cousin Ashley. She's always getting over on them, but not me, cause she's just the way I was.

On the face of it, this is a fairly good freshman essay, especially for an in-class effort. As I have already noted, the introduction needs a better focus, since it really lists too many theses, whether children are smarter than adults, whether they get away with murder because they are cute and adorable or because they are smart, or favorites, or pitiful. She also creates some confusion between her own experiences, general experiences, and her relationship with Corsica. On the other hand, the logic is there, even if it is somewhat obscure, and with a bit of revising, the paragraph could be made clear and focused. Shanique takes an interesting tack in the conclusion, by contrasting her adult self with her childhood self and by showing how the myth of her angelic character persists even though she is now willing to confess. The last sentence, showing how children like Ashley continue to fool adults, gives the essay a universal quality. The very last sentence is one of the few that captures Shanique's voice, and it is one of the best in the essay: "She's always getting over on them, but not me, cause she's just the way I was." Another very good descriptive sentence occurs in paragraph one: "I was a skinny little girl with big eyes and a deep voice."

However, there are few other such strong sentences. The middle paragraph starts with a stiff phrase Shanique would never use in speech, "Upon remembering our childhood," which results, as such a construction almost inevitably does, in a dangling modifier. In this paragraph Shanique's collapsing of the cat and the chicken stories is confusing because so many narrative details are lost, which leads, perhaps, to the horror one instructor expressed in her comments to me, "What concerns me most in this narrative is the picture Shanique presents of herself. I don't think she realizes how strongly her matter-of-fact and rather emotionless comments about the chickens and the cat . . . will affect the reader." Shanique's phrase "the death of my grandfather's chickens" just does not come across as humorous, although I suspect she meant it to because of her addition of "As for the cat, no one likes cats anyways, but my grandmother was not pleased with the fact that we decided to dispose of the cat in her wood-burning heater." Imagining Shanique speaking these lines confirms that she could only have meant them as a joke, but of course a reader would never know this. Thus, with the essential elements that comprise her unique voice, intonation and the use of BEV, restricted, Shanique cannot meet the demands of academic prose.

Without the covert prestige of BEV, her toughness and meanness come across to some readers as shocking cruelty. Little of the humor comes across, and the reader is less likely to remember that Shanique is writing about an instance when she was an irresponsible child. Even a reading of the transcript, without the benefit of Shanique's mimicry and intonation, can decrease the humor and increase our tendency to judge her character negatively. I have no doubt that an academic who is unfamiliar with BEV culture and folklore will be far less able to perceive the clever, cool, mean ethos Shanique is assuming here and will primarily be startled and perhaps offended by the image of a cruel, very improper, little girl. Although an academic unfamiliar with BEV might understand Shanique's mean ethos if she were to tell her story, it seems to be lost in the writing.

For example, in at least one instructor's eyes she appears cruel and unthinking rather than funny and tough; in terms of classical rhetoric, she is suspected of having bad character. Although toughness is valued in academia as well as in the BEV speaking community, expressions of toughness are markedly different. An academic does not claim to have beaten up an opponent, although she may very well "pummel" him in academic debate (metaphorically, of course). Shanique's pride in her independence and toughness, her claim to getting over on the adults because of her wits, and her ritual revenge on the chicken and the cat, even if she had included all the details of the spoken version, may be completely misunderstood or overlooked by an academic audience.

Her ethos in her expository writing is also problematic. As I explained in the opening to this chapter, the ethos she constructs in her essay on hazing is evaluated by the instructors as uncommitted to the topic, not concerned with or knowledgeable about the issues. In their view, she displays neither good will nor good sense, although her character does not come into question, as it did in the narrative. The full text of her essay follows:

> In order to join a fraternity or sorority pledges are literally put through hell. Is it all worth it? When asked, most inactive members agree that it was probably not worth it and wouldn't go through with it again. However when asked if they tested pledges in a difficult manner, all agreed that they had, but couldn't give specific reasons as to why. So to become a member of such organizations one must be willing to put up with a lot of unnecessary anxiety, embarrassment and sometimes even physical as well as mental pain.
>
> In my opinion, physical pain is quite unnecessary. In some cases mental anguish and embarrassment is also unnecessary. These acts do not prove a person's loyalty to the organization it only proves that these persons are able to put up with stupid traditions and minor invasions of their rights.
>
> It is also my opinion that the pledgees should know when they've reached their limit in doing something and not be afraid to quit. I'm not too sure about all frats and soros, but I do know that all the predominately Black organizations are not allowed to make a pledge "drop line", the once a person has gone "on line" then the decision to drop is solely up to him. Therefore, I feel that the pledgee should know his limitations and know when to stop an act.
>
> It is also my opinion that the pledgers should be aware that undo mental and physical anguish does not prove that a person will be loyal to the sisterhood or brotherhood of the organization and

should test the pledges on loyalty and not mental stability and physical stamina. Since I really haven't thought about this business of
pledging too much, I really haven't thought of a solution, but I sure if
people would sit down and think of an alternative to hazing a poor
pledge to death.

Surprisingly, Shanique wrote this essay after our lively conversation about hazing. One of its most notable aspects is the weak
ethos, especially the way she backs away from having thought
about the issue in the conclusion. As one instructor puts it, "The
closing acknowledgment of thoughtlessness undermines what little credibility has been established." The transcript from our conversation shows she actually does suggest at least two solutions
at that time. Similarly, the transition sentences for all the paragraphs are of the hedging variety: "In my opinion" or "It is also
my opinion that." Although Shanique is indeed giving her opinion, this phrase has an air of apology, as does her statement that
she is "not too sure about all frats and soros." She could certainly
make a case without having such detailed knowledge and without weakening the reader's trust in her good sense.

On the other hand, considered as an in-class draft, this essay
shows promise. For example, in spite of some errors in grammar
and some shifting of pronouns from "one" to "they" to "a person,"
the language, both diction and syntax, can be quite sophisticated.
She writes "So, to become a member of such organizations one
must be willing to put up with a lot of unnecessary anxiety,
embarrassment, and sometimes even physical as well as mental
pain." And some sentences show strong and interesting voice, as
the opening, "In order to join a fraternity or sorority pledges are
literally put through hell." One instructor, perhaps hearing this
sophistication and the honesty of opinion, states "clearly written
sentences—a very natural, matter-of-fact style." The same instructor found her voice "sincere."

Yet weaknesses in the language of this essay detract from
Shanique's ethos for some instructors. Some words come
directly from informal discourse, for example, "frats and soros"
or "drop line" and "on line." Interestingly, she puts the last two
phrases in quotes yet does not define them, although one
instructor commented that she "does not understand what [they]
mean." In other words, Shanique assumes knowledge that her

friends might have, or that an interlocutor in casual conversation might request, but that a reader of an academic essay, who demands specificity and accuracy, might be at a loss for. She also uses shifting terminology, as in "pledgees" and "pledges," displaying what could easily be read as carelessness by readers who expect consistent terminology. But the real trouble with this essay stems from gaps in the development, gaps that Shanique has supplied in detail in her conversation with me about hazing. By adding these details, she would present a very different ethos: she would appear more committed, more concerned, and more knowledgeable.

To illustrate, I present the conversation, which is very long, in sections, in the order in which they occur, and make comparisons to the essay as I progress. It will become apparent that Shanique once again is able to draw on intonation and BEV, and on her ethos as a "mean" and independent woman, to strengthen her arguments.

Valerie: What's your view of hazing? Why don't you take a stand, for or against, or whatever?

Shanique: I think, I, I, personally, I'm against it [hazing] because some people are kind of weak, especially mental hazing because I think, okay, that like, forcing somebody to drink, I think they must kind of sort of want to drink, too because ya, after a while you say "I can't take it anymore" and just take a stand and, I mean, if, if they're going to try to force you to do stuff that, why would you want to be a part of a group of people who won't let you think on your own? But mental hazing, I think that's, that's kind of bad because I couldn't, . . . just ignore stuff, 'cause when people are . . . coming down hard on me, just fussing at me and stuff, if I don't think . . . it's fair, I just ignore 'em and start talking about other things. Like if they going to be in my face, just, just talking about me, just putting me down and everything, and I can just be . . . looking straight at 'em, but I don't hear a word they're saying. But I know everybody can't do that. 'Cause, 'cause I just look at people and it's just like, and after a while they'll know I'm not listening, 'cause they'll say "Are you listening to me?" And I was going (*listlessly*) "Yeah, yeah." (*laughs*) And 'cause . . . for people to do that, they shouldn't want to torture people like that. 'Cause messing with somebody's mind is serious, and I don't, I mean, I don't think it's right to do something like that, and I think they should be prosecuted. If they can be proven to do it. 'Cause, 'cause mental hazing, you have no proof . . .

Valerie: Um hum.

Shanique: 'Cause you can't, unless, I mean, unless you had a recorder . . .

Valerie: (*laughs*) Yeah.

Shanique: on you or something.

Valerie: Yeah.

Shanique: That's the only way you could prove it. But if they were like hazing you mentally, then you should, like, you shouldn't want to be on that part, want that either. 'Cause you want to, 'cause I would think they trying to brainwash me into believe a certain way and to be intimi–, I don't, I try not to be intimidated by people 'cause if it's somebody who's, just like, (*sighs*) I dunno, but, um, I, if I can't handle it then, I'm just not, I just try not to get into situations that I can't handle. But I think the person that's being hazed, I think they should report it if they have proof, but, like, if, um (*long pause*)

Valerie: Well, proof would also be if they could get someone to admit . . .

Shanique: Yeah. Somebody else, if they had a witness to admit it for them, then I think that would be pretty good, too. Because then they both may have been mentally hazed. But I don't think that they should haze a person anyways. I mean, like when you pledging do a few things, I mean, I don't think, I personally don't think that somebody should get hit 'cause if I get hit I intend to hit that person back. It's just a natural reaction.

Valerie: Um hum.

In this first section of our conversation Shanique takes up the idea of mental hazing after I introduce the topic. She needs no prompting to state her opinion. It is, in fact, quite in keeping with the mean ethos she has consistently presented: that pledges have the primary responsibility to decide if they are willing to submit to hazing. They should know better than to do something that would harm them, and they should have second thoughts about joining an organization that harasses them. She uses a vivid personal example of how she ignores people who try to fluster her, who "fuss at" her, a passive resistance tactic that she finds effective. However, she recognizes that "everybody can't do that." Then she comes right out and condemns mental hazing as "wrong" and says those who can be proved to be doing it should be punished. This observation leads her to consider what would constitute proof, and she concludes that witnesses or even a tape would be best. At this point our attention is drawn to the recorder, but it does not interfere with Shanique's train of thought. She restates that pledges should stay in control and not be intimidated, and, using herself as an example again, states further that they should defend themselves against physical violence.

The personal involvement and personal examples contrast sharply with the ethos constructed in the essay. The statement that pledges are responsible, a very strong opinion, evidently, does not occur in the essay until the end of paragraph three. In the essay, moreover, the statement is unsupported, while at this point in the conversation she has shown vividly how she herself deals with mental intimidation and harassment. The conversation continues:

Shanique: And I think that, like my aunt, she pledged, when she was going to school, she went to a school in east Texas, and she pledged a sorority, and she pledged a lot a fratern-, uh, uh, honor society things, and when she was pledging a sorority she said that the things, the kind of stuff that they did was like, sh-, they would like tell them something stupid like "Bring me an empty glass of water," and you'd have to figure out what that was, (*Valerie laughs*) I mean, figure out how to do it, or like they would ask you to do their laundry or something to just, uh, take up some time. But she say most of the time they had, they had to go to the library and make sure they kept up with a high GPA, and I don't under-, I don't understand what happen 'cause I was thinking about pledging the same sorority that she pledged, 'cause I would be a legacy. . . . And so I was going, (*tsk*) after I saw some of the girls on this campus that are in that sorority, they're pretty nice but at times they act so stuck up . . . and they don't never do anything kind of stuff, and I heard some other people talking about when they pledge they be telling you, like, "You have to go and do this." Like you have to go and sleep with this certain guy. And I'm going, "Ohhh K, I don't think so." And, and you, you have to, have to go to all these parties, and you have to get drunk, if you don't get drunk, I say, some people just can't handle alcohol, some people just don't like to drink.

Valerie: Yeah.

Shanique: 'Cause I just don't like to drink alcohol, 'cause I like to be in control of my situation. I say, what's the purpose of having fun if you can't remember it the next day? And so, I don't, I mean, I think people sh-, they should kind of look into a sorority, or fraternity before they start pledging . . . and try to ask some, some older people on campus, I mean, they're not going to know exactly what happen 'cause they're, 'cause sororities and fraternities are kind of secretive when they're pledging and stuff and actives aren't supposed to tell what they had to go through to become, but I know most of the people that I've asked that have pledged, they say, "Well, I can't tell you what we did, but if I had to do it over again, I probably would not have pledged, 'cause some of the stuff is stupid." And I think it's, some of it is unnecessary.

In this section Shanique considers some very concrete alternatives to what she considers harmful hazing, although she only makes clear that she considers them acceptable later in the conversation, and she also mentions the enduring charges of sorority snobbery. Again, her voice is interesting, and strong, as when she uses direct quotation to tell about her aunt's experiences. She also gives concrete and vivid examples of inappropriate hazing and her reaction to it (saying no), and reiterates the value of being "in control of my situation." Finally, she discusses some options for the person considering pledging.

In comparison to her essay, she is far more specific in this section about what constitutes improper and proper hazing and presents a more balanced view by implying that some hazing can be acceptable. Compare paragraph two in her essay, where her only statement about acceptable hazing is "In some cases mental anguish and embarrassment is also unnecessary." We will see as the conversation continues just what she means. The most striking difference to me, however, is that in the conversation she reports exactly what she asks inactive members and gives a direct quote representing their answers. In contrast, in her essay she does not even make clear who asked: "When asked, most inactive members agree that it was probably not worth it and wouldn't go through it again. However, when asked if they tested pledges in a difficult manner, all agreed that they had, but couldn't give specific reasons as to why." The spoken version presents a credible ethos, a college student getting some inside information from friends. The written version, in contrast, leaves readers wondering what kind of poll was taken, who took it, and what "a difficult manner" means. It is impersonal and imprecise, mimicking academic language but not really meeting its standards.

The next section of the conversation moves to the positive side of hazing, why it may be useful and what kinds of hazing are acceptable. Shanique also presents a good alternative to hazing.

Valerie: You think any of it is necessary? Or . . .
Shanique: Yeah, I think it's, I think it's mostly unnecessary. I think, like, if the person, ah, but it's a kind of way of weeding out people, too,

'cause like you say, "Well, if they can, if they are willing to do this to be a part of us, then we'll know that they'll be a, a participant in the club. 'Cause if you have it free for everybody to join, then you have a few people just hanging on, and they'll get all the pleasures, but they won't do any of the hard work . . . to get into it." But I don't think it should be something really hard . . .

Valerie: Yeah.

Shanique: Or really stupid.

Valerie: Is there a, maybe a better way they could weed people out, too? I mean, maybe they're weeding out people who can think for themselves as well (*laughs*).

Shanique: Yeah, (*laughs*) 'cause that's what I said my problem would be when we were pledging, when I was pledging, 'cause some of my friends wanted me to pledge with them, but I said, "That might be a mistake, 'cause I'm kind of stubborn. And if they tell me to do something I may not want to do it, and y'all, y'all'll get in trouble, and you might hate me." They said "Well, but then it might work for the best. Maybe they won't be so hard on us (*both laugh*) if they just knew they had to put up with you all the time." I said, "Oh." But, um, I don't know of any other, I don't really know 'cause I don't know what they do, but I, I think, like, I think it's okay sometimes for them to dress alike 'cause sometime when they're pledging they dress alike, . . . and I think it's, I mean, and sometimes, like, do service projects . . .

Valerie: Sure.

Shanique: 'Cause I think that's just great.

Valerie: Yeah.

Shanique: Like maybe, maybe let them on a trial or something and have them, to see what the club is all about.

Valerie: Yeah.

Shanique: Like, like give you two weeks to, uh, see what, like, these are the service projects that we do and kind of like Girl Scouts, like everybody can join Girl Scouts. (*Valerie laughs*) You have to earn so many merits and stuff before you can move into the next level.

Valerie: Yeah.

Shanique: I think that would be great. And, and, be able to do service work and, and their fun activities and try to keep a good GPA. And they'll know that you're a person that's worthy of it, and you're not taking on more than you can handle. But to put people through a lot of mental trauma is sad.

Again Shanique enlivens her account and strengthens her argument by using quotes, this time telling about her stubborn nature and her unwillingness to do anything she does not want to do. This statement takes us back, of course, to her original point. It seems remarkable that she could have written in her essay "Since I really haven't thought about this business of pledging too much, I really haven't thought of a solution" when she has stated in our conversation two solutions, alternative activities like dressing alike or letting everyone pledge and earn points toward full rank, like in Girl Scouts. In the conclusion of her essay she does say the pledges should be tested on loyalty, but she does not explain how. In this section of the conversation she gives one concrete method.

In the section that follows, Shanique, prompted by my questions, gives another concrete method for improving hazing. She also uses narrative to show how brutal hazing can be:

Shanique: 'Cause one of my friends told me he pledged a fraternity at Lamar, . . . and he was telling me that this other fraternity was pledging, and most of the guys in that fraternity were like, look like football players. They were huge. And it was this little scrawny guy (*Valerie laughs*), and they were beating up on the poor little guy and put him in the hospital.

Valerie: Oh God.

Shanique: But, and, he couldn't figure it out, so he went, after he got out of the hospital he went right back online, and started . . .

Valerie: Oh noo!

Shanique: Pledging again. And then they took him over. And I was going, "I wouldn't a went through that," 'cause they broke his collar bone while he was pledging.

Valerie: Oh God!

Shanique: So I said, they should have been put on probation. But they said somehow they kept it a secret. I would have had, I would have told. I couldn't a went through that much pain.

Valerie: I think the reason they get away with it is people don't, they don't . . .

Shanique: Yeah, they're afraid. 'Cause they say, "Well, if I tell then they know I'm chicken."

Valerie: Yeah.

Shanique: Say, I'm not afraid to be chicken. Ever.

Valerie: Yeah. It looks like the opposite, doesn't it?

Shanique: Umm.

Valerie: Some people, they don't tell 'cause they're afraid, really.

Shanique: Mmmm.

Valerie: So you think the University should have a role in trying to prevent . . .

Shanique: Yeah.

Valerie: Hazing?

Shanique: Yeah. They should, and they should have a council where all, like something where they all meet or something, and say "This is what you can do, and this is what you can't do. And if we find out, then you'll be put on probation." Do it like that. 'Cause I think a lot of the stuff that some people go through is unnecessary.

Obviously, Shanique's essay would have greatly benefited from an example of physical hazing and the pain that can result. In fact, one instructor noted "I'm not sure what she means about 'physical pain is quite unnecessary' until further down in the paragraph. She means pain associated with hazing." This reader could have gotten the point much more easily if Shanique had mentioned the example she gives me in conversation.

The next section shows that Shanique not only takes the issue of hazing seriously but is actually considering pledging herself.

Shanique: And I'm thinking about pledging in the fall, so . . . (*both laugh*)

Valerie: Oh no. I pity the women who have to take you, (*Shanique laughs*) make you do anything. (*laughs*)

Shanique: I was, I, but I'm, I'm not sure which sorority I want to pledge. Because my aunt is one, and she said, well, when she went to school "We did, we did, like, volunteered at the hospital, and we did, we tutored students, and we went to the nursing homes."

Valerie: Great.

Shanique: "And took fruit baskets and stuff." And, and they helped the Salvation Army, and they did all this stuff. And she said, "But then of course we had our parties, and . . . we had all our parties, and we went, like on Spring Break a lot of us got together and went places and stuff, and we did like this." And then, I come down here, and I never see them doing anything but walking around campus with their noses in the air, if it rain, they drown. And I say (*both laugh*) "they just, they're just not the same, somehow." She say, she say, "I guess it change with the times" whatever happen, I mean.

Valerie: So you're looking for one, sorority, that can . . .

Shanique: Yeah.

Valerie: Be like that.

Shanique: Yeah. That's kind of what I want. But sh-, she say if I pledge, then she would finance me like little dresses and everything we'd get together and all that silly stuff you have to buy, like, one sorority, they call themselves ducks before they go, before they become the one, they have to carry these little ducks around. They're "ducks on the move" and they have to carry their ducks and their suitcases around everywhere that they go. (*laughs*) And she say she could help me out like that (*laughs*) if I pledge, and I thought that was kind of cute.

Valerie: Yeah.

Shanique: But, uh, I mean, stuff like that, that would be okay.

Valerie: Yeah.

Shanique: Because, so, 'cause people going to be looking at you and laughing, . . . but I don't mind being laughed at. I laugh, too. . . . But some stuff is kind of stupid.

Valerie: Yeah. Some stuff. Like what kind of stuff is stupid?

Shanique: Like forcing, like forcing a person, like, um, this one guy told me his sister was pledging a sorority, and she, and one a, and a Big, they call them Big Sisters, she and her Big Sister were shopping, and her Big Sister saw this dress and said, "You have to buy me that dress."

Valerie: Oh my God.

Shanique: And I say, no, they say, "Buy me that dress," and I would say, "Give me the money," I go take it off the rack and I get out. That's what I call buying. (*Valerie laughs*) They mean, like, take the money out of your own pocket, and I say, now that's stupid. . . . They just have to, they, but, um, one thing I know about black soror-, I don't know if white sororities do this, but like, if you can make it on line, then they can't make you quit. You're the only person who can decide to quit. . . . I say, so that's all I needed to know. They tell me to do something, I say "Uh uh. Sorry." That's stupid.

Valerie: Yeah.

Shanique: Hmm. Like, buy me a dress, and it's like a hundred and seventy dollars.

Valerie: You know, I'm sure even if it was five dollars you wouldn't do it.

Shanique: Um hum! That's right! . . . I say I'm not going to get any wear out of it.

Valerie: Yeah.

Shanique: So, and, and, um, I think it's kind of, I mean it can make a person kind of wonder if you want to be in the sorority 'cause, like, when you're on line they're all coming down hard on you and everything, but then when you finally make it into the sorority, they're like sisters, and you have to wonder, like, Does she really like me? Is she really my friend, or is she just doing this just because I was lucky enough and made it over? Kind of like makes you wonder.

Valerie: Yeah, that makes me wonder, too.

Shanique: Sometimes I wonder if it's worth it. So I, I, I kind want to pledge, but I'm kind of reluctant to, also.

Valerie: What are your positive reasons for wanting to pledge?

Shanique: Because, this sorority that I want to pledge, they do do a lot of service projects and stuff, and then they always. Oh. The main reason I want to pledge is because I want to step in a Greek show. . . . 'Cause I just love to dance.

Valerie: Oh yeah!

Shanique: and I want everybody to see me! (*laughs*)

Valerie: Yeah, that's good stuff.

Shanique: That's my main reason. 'Cause I love Greek shows. . . . And I would love to step. And then, then, I also, having a sisterhood, like always having somebody to talk to. But I always do anyway. (*Valerie laughs*) 'Cause I have Laurie! (*both laugh*) She's always willing to listen. And, um, and then they kind of, they always do stuff together, and like, when they have parties and stuff. It's kind, it's more fun when you, when you're one of them when you're at parties and stuff.

At this point, as we are running short on time and Shanique shows no sign of exhausting the topic, I change it to minority recruitment and retention.

Once again in the section above she considers in concrete terms what kind of hazing is acceptable and what is unacceptable. She shows a more balanced view by discussing the positive aspects of sororities, such as the friendship, fun, and service work, as well as the negative, such as the snobbery. The stories about "ducks on the move" and the demand for a pledge to buy a dress are yet two more concrete examples of the type conspicuously missing from her essay. Likewise, her humorous use of the maxim about snobs drowning from holding their noses in the air ("if it rain, they drown") emphasizes the lack of life in the essay. In the spoken version, she shows personal involvement in the issue, not just through her aunt or her friends but also because she wants to join a sorority herself, which is highlighted by her discussion of her aunt's willingness to "finance" her. She also hints at another way to develop her topic when she discusses the possible real feelings of actives toward pledges.

The ethos Shanique constructs in this section is consistent with the strong and independent image she constructs in all the interviews. Her unique reason for wanting to pledge, to be seen, to perform, to celebrate and have a good time, expresses an ethos that, if we could understand it, would certainly win our good will. Her vitality and her intelligence should inform her academic writing as they do her speaking. If they are lost, we cannot really know who she is or where she comes from.

Yet the accommodation will have to be mostly on her side. The chances of academia learning to accept her ethos as it stands are slim. The challenge for teachers of writing—especially academic writing—is to help Shanique and others whose rhetoric may be influenced by the conventions of different discourse communities conform to the academic models and yet retain their identity. We have yet to accept this challenge, much less to meet it.

Notes

[1]From the folk poem, "Shine."

Talking Respectable: Superpolite Strategies for Saving Face and Keeping Peace

Shanique's ethos is primarily "mean"; to achieve this, she draws heavily on the "bad" smart talking tradition. In contrast, Laurie cultivates a ladylike ethos, drawing upon "respectable" and "proper" language. Graciousness and politeness are important to Laurie's ethos, as important as independence and toughness are to Shanique's. Whether Laurie is the passive "naive" type, easily swayed by male sweet talking, as described by Abrahams ("Negotiating Respect" 73) is unclear from the texts collected here. However, she is far from passive in interaction with female peers. She offers her opinions freely, yet gently and politely, and she actively maintains a respectable public front for herself and for her interlocutors. In short, she follows a code of respectable, ladylike behavior. She makes it abundantly clear what, in her opinion, constitutes such behavior.

I found my initial impression of Laurie's ethos reinforced by her use of certain discourse strategies which a number of researchers have noted as stereotypically associated with femininity (Lakoff, *Language;* Coates; Hill). Most notably, she employs a great many superpolite forms. Lakoff, somewhat impressionistically, introduces the notion of superpolite forms; working-class speakers may strive for "better" English in order to be identified with middle-class values: "it's considered more mannerly in middle-class society to speak 'properly'" (55). As a result, hypercorrection often marks superpolite speech. However, superpoliteness is linguistically manifested in many ways besides hypercorrection:

> [W]omen don't use off-color or indelicate expressions; women are the experts at euphemism; more positively, women are the repositories of tact and know the right things to say to other people, while men carelessly blurt out whatever they are thinking. Women are supposed to be particularly careful to say "please" and "thank-you" and to uphold the other social conventions; certainly a woman who fails

at these tasks is apt to be in more trouble than a man who does so: in a man it's "just like a man," and indulgently overlooked unless his behavior is really boorish. In a woman it's social death in conventional circles to refuse to go by the rules. (55–56)

Lakoff overstates her case to make her point (not all men are blurters, but Shanique sometimes is). Coates criticizes Lakoff for relying on intuition and unsystematic observation rather than on empirical investigation. O'Barr and Atkins criticize her identification of superpolite features with women; in empirical studies of witnesses' language during trials, they identified these features with powerlessness or lack of experience in the courtroom.

Laurie's use of superpolite forms is so noticeable as to have forced itself on my attention. Whether this arises from her identification with femininity or with powerlessness is impossible to declare. At any rate, while specific linguistic features have yet to be identified with gender, researchers agree that women's language is stereotyped as distinct from men's. In this respect, Laurie's language behavior, both what she says and how she says it, leads me to conjecture that she has a strong image of how a lady should speak and that she often tries to be identified with that image by imitating that way of speaking (Le Page and Tabouret-Keller). The African-American tradition of "proper" or "respectable" language, associated with feminine values and with the home and school (discussed in Chapter 2) may influence Laurie in this regard.

Specifically, Laurie's stereotypical feminine language takes the following forms:

1. She bowdlerizes language and frequently uses mild, quaint expletives like "goodness" and "dang";
2. She goes to some pains to practice tact, often saving face for her interlocutors even when it might not be necessary;
3. Similarly, she frequently accentuates the positive and strives to cooperate with and bolster her interlocutor;
4. She frequently uses conventional formulas for politeness such as "thank you" and "excuse me," even in situations so friendly and informal that it would not be expected; and
5. She hedges, especially in her writing, seemingly to avoid confrontation or strong self-assertion.

None of these features are unique to Laurie. For example, Shanique also says "dang," and most writers hedge occasionally.

It is not the exclusive use of these features that marks Laurie's discourse as "ladylike," but rather the combination of these features, their frequency, and the impression created by talking about being a lady.

The clearest example of Laurie's identification with ladylike language is her avoidance of taboo words; she seldom uses any obscenity, a trait which is almost universally believed to be distasteful to ladies (though we have no evidence to show whether this stereotype is grounded in actual practice). She occasionally uses "pisses off" in the sense of "angers" but that is about as graphic as she gets. The expletives "dang" and "shoot," and the surprisingly quaint "oh my goodness!" are more common to her vocabulary, as are "my goodness!" and "oh my goodness gracious!" Although none of the informants, male or female, uses much taboo language and Shanique also uses "shoot" and "dang," only Laurie uses the almost stereotypically ladylike "goodness" expletives.

The other strategies listed above can best be seen holistically in the texts, both spoken and written, Laurie produced for this study. They not only exemplify her superpoliteness and tendency to hedge but also show how frequently she introduces the topic of femininity, thus directing her interlocutors' attention to it and, like the other informants, attempting to manipulate others' perceptions of her. Comments that Laurie makes in conversations with me or with Shanique create the impression that she has a very distinct stereotype of feminine language and behavior in mind. For example, in conversations with me, Laurie offers decided opinions about male/female behavior. A striking occurrence arises in our discussion of hazing:

> As far as guys, . . . most guys are wilder than girls anyway and . . . it's like having you sleep around with all different girls and, I mean, that's cool to guys. But I, I don't think a girl, a sorority that's trying to represent what a lady should be, I don't, I don't, I've never heard of any, you know, making you go around sleeping with guys. To be in that sorority and stuff like drinking. And getting drunk.

Laurie uses the word "lady" explicitly here, in a way that suggests she has a stereotype of a lady in mind.

In another instance, she reveals to Shanique that she does not believe women should initiate dating:

Laurie: It's harder for a girl, I mean, you, you really have to wait till a guy asks you for your number. . . . I don't be wanting to ask "You want my number?" I may be thinking, "Man, please ask me, please ask me." (*both laughing loudly*)

Shanique: I'm just like this, "You want my number?"

Laurie: 'Cause I'm enjoying this conversation. I want to talk to you again. Then you don't be knowing when you're going to see them again. And you just be hoping. (*Shanique laughing*) Dang!

This stretch of conversation emphasizes the difference between the two women. Shanique's style is to ask directly ("I'm just like this, 'You want my number?'"), while Laurie believes she has to wait passively for the man to initiate. Evidently, maintaining respectable social conventions is quite important to her, and the unspoken is as important as the spoken.

The conversation likewise exemplifies Laurie's tendency to put interlocutors' needs first, to accentuate the positive, and to serve as a facilitator. To understand how she does this, some context for this passage must be provided. At the point where we enter this conversation, Shanique had just told Laurie about an incident in which she dared a male friend to ask a strange woman for a date; he, in turn, had dared her to approach an athlete for the same purpose. Both took up the challenge, but he won, since he managed to elicit a phone number. Laurie responds to the story by reviving Shanique's ego: "It's harder for a girl," she consoles. Perhaps she is also signifying, albeit mildly, on Shanique, for having approached the man in the first place. The fact that she elucidates etiquette at this point raises the possibility.

In other comments about male/female relationships, Laurie displays her expectation that courting males be appropriately gentlemanly. She is particularly impressed by being walked home. Of one young man she approvingly confides that "He toted my umbrella for me." Another young man treated her very badly, and she reports to Shanique that she chided him, but her chiding is exceedingly mild. She leaves his room indignantly, telling him she will walk herself home; she observes to Shanique, "I don't even know if I said bye. I think I did say bye." She ends her story by claiming that she will not sit next to the offender in class. Shanique (or Divinity) would have probably threatened to break his neck. This is another instance of the importance Laurie places on maintaining respectable social conventions.

On three occasions, Shanique explicitly comments upon, and gently pokes fun at, Laurie's construction of herself as ladylike. At one point, Laurie sniffles and says quietly, "Excuse me." Shanique marks (imitates) her, in an even quieter tone, "Excuse me!" and they laugh. At another point, Laurie is explaining that she believes romantic involvements often begin as friendships. She comments, in a very soft voice, about her chances with one young man, "I think I'm a nice person and I think he's a nice person." Then more loudly, beginning to laugh, she adds, "And I think two nice people should be together!" After both laugh for a few seconds, Shanique marks Laurie, softening her voice, exaggerating and imitating her tones: "(*Tsk*) I think I'm a nice person, (*tsk*) and I think he's a nice person, too." The signifying isn't lost on Laurie, and both of them laugh heartily at her "niceness." In their laughter they apparently acknowledge that Laurie's philosophy of niceness is a shallow justification for her desire to be with this male. In the final instance, Shanique is telling Laurie about a male friend of hers. He met Laurie once and hardly spoke to her, but he spoke to Shanique about the meeting: as Shanique reports it to Laurie, "He just thought you looked nice." Laurie responds to Shanique, "Thank you!" almost as if she were talking to the young man. In mock sarcasm, Shanique replies, "Oh God!" Laurie counters with "Oh goodness" in a falling intonation, and Shanique, after a brief pause and some hesitations and false starts, changes the subject.

Laurie's attempt to sound respectable may have some undesired rhetorical effects on her written texts, for example, making her sound unassertive or unsure of her ideas. While on the whole she proves competent at constructing an effective ethos in argument, she emphasizes respectability by showing herself to be humble, especially by hedging. She avoids a polemic tone and instead cultivates a reasonable, eminently fair voice—reminiscent of the raceless strategy observed by Fordham, by which African-American students may invest a great deal of sincere trust in middle-class values of equality and fairness, ignoring that racial and class prejudice can hamper them.

The text of the essay, below, illustrates my points:

To Be or Not To Be a Greek

Many college students want to be in a sorority or fraternity. Yet, to be a member of such "prestigious" organizations, you must pay the cost.

Initiations determine if you really have the qualifications to be in this group. Or rather they prove what all you are willing to do to be accepted.

To be honest, I wonder if the initiations are really worth going through to be accepted. As a non-greek, I am merely looking in from the outside. Yet, I have caught tired glimpses on many girls faces while pledging to be in a fraternity. I have seen their so called "big sisters" openly ridicule them in public. For instance, the other night at a Greek show, the girls pledging to become AKA's had to stand in line from shortest to tallest with their hands folded. They all had to either look down or look to the side. Then their "big sisters" would come up to them and have them do all kind of things.

On the whole, I don't think people should have to be initiated to join certain organizations. Actually, I just can not understand why these organizations do not accept you for who you are. Instead of making you prove that you want to be a part of them. Ironically, your "big sisters" treat you as if you're very insignificant while pledging. Yet, the moment your pledging period is over and you have "succeeded," they then treat you as if you really belong with them. Right now, I have decided not to be a Greek. But perhaps, tomorrow I'll reconsider. Because right now, I'm merely looking in from the outside.

Laurie expresses her views somewhat indirectly, avoiding aggression or polemics. A very striking feature of her written argument is her use of metaphor and irony. By portraying herself as someone looking in from outside, she suggests objectivity. By being ironic, she positions herself against the "unreasonable" opposing side. However, her argument is weak in some of the same ways that Shanique's is, particularly because it lacks sufficient detail, detail that does appear in her spoken version, although often it is prompted by my questions. In other words, she is apparently unaware that by providing detail she will bolster her argument and strengthen her attempt to appear reasonable. In this respect she simply reveals her novice status as an academic writer.

Unfortunately, she is not finally willing to take a strong stand. Although she dares to be ironic and to challenge the hypocrisy of the sororities, she ends by hedging, essentially drawing on a superpolite strategy. She admits her view, as an outsider, may be defective, and says she may reconsider it. Her move is conciliatory and not without value in argument, although it rather weakens her stance by its position at the end of the essay. However, what is most important to note is that it upholds her attempt to construct a ladylike ethos.

In the end, Laurie's efforts to smooth out social rough spots often work against her. Lakoff put the dilemma for ladies well in her groundbreaking treatment of the subject: "a girl is damned if she does, damned if she doesn't":

> If she refuses to talk like a lady, she is ridiculed and subjected to criticism as unfeminine; if she does learn, she is ridiculed as unable to think clearly, unable to take part in a serious discussion: in some sense, as less than fully human. (*Language and Women's Place* 6)

Thus, Shanique may seem too independent and aggressive, Laurie too polite and passive. Neither stance hits the nail on the head in terms of the conventions of academic discourse.

Talking Respectable/Talking Bad

There is a fundamental tension between respectable talk and BEV (Chapters 1 and 2), arising from the association of education and success with SAE. BEV thus becomes equated with talking bad in general. Unfortunately, Laurie's apparently unselfconscious use of spoken BEV works against her desire to construct a ladylike image. The problem seldom occurs in her writing, although at least one instance of informal and spontaneous writing, a note she left me before I began the study, contains BEV. It provides a good example of her occasional juxtaposition of superpolite forms and BEV:

> Valerie,
> I came by to see [you], but you wasn't in. I just wanted to know when you will need us to help you on your thesis. Call me when you have the time. Thanks! [in very large letters]

The omission of the first "you" is a common mistake in hurried writing, but the shift into informal dialect ("you wasn't in") seems of a different order. In a situation such as this one, in which informants do not share a knowledge of BEV yet are fairly well-acquainted, we would expect Laurie to monitor her speech by avoiding BEV. Notice that Laurie's use of my first name shows that she feels confident and somewhat familiar with me, although we are on a semi-formal footing because of my higher status (as a teacher). Furthermore, BEV is a dialect normally spoken, not written. Thus, Laurie's use of BEV in this note is either a slip or a deliberate manipulation of style. It certainly appears to be an accidental use of informal dialect—not a deliberate attempt to sound informal or "African-American." Other evidence, particularly Laurie's later revealed surprise at hearing herself use BEV on tape, supports my intuition that this phrase is a slip, in the sense that it is an unconscious shift into BEV when the writer meant to use SAE.

Overall, the note reinforces a teacher/student relationship. Laurie gives me the clear signal that she considers my time valuable, and she adds a hint of self-abasement, most apparent in the sentence "I *just* wanted to know when *you* will *need us*," (my emphasis) not, for example, "I wanted you to know when I could be available to you." The "Thanks!" has a similar effect—since she is doing me a favor—yet, on a positive note, it adds to the graciousness of her ethos.

Among the tendencies researchers note in stereotypically feminine language are an avoidance of nonstandard forms, especially in situations where there is an attempt to construct a positive ethos (Lakoff, *Language;* Coates). According to this research, then, the females in this study, at least if they are interested, like Laurie, in constructing a ladylike ethos, would avoid BEV forms, possibly producing hypercorrect forms in the attempt. Laurie does not display hypercorrection, but her tapes reveal frequent instances of BEV in her conversations with me. For example, she consistently pronounces "ask" as "axed" and use the "it is" expletive where in SAE "there is" would be expected (as in "it's a lot of blacks out there" and "I think it's other ways that they can cut off their taxes"). Other examples of her use of BEV, all from her conversation with me, are listed below:

1. I don't think it's anything wrong with it.
2. I have went to a few rush-, well, one rush for a sorority.
3. We was about to pass the park.
4. I didn't know where it had came from.
5. My teacher name was Miss Bitner.
6. But I don't be stealing.

These statements must be considered in light of the fact that Laurie attended predominantly African-American schools until she came to the university. They show that she is comfortable with

BEV. They do not show that she is incapable of speaking SAE, for most of her spoken discourse is SAE. And her writing is almost exclusively SAE, which is why she should be classified as bidialectal in spite of the fact that she sometimes produces BEV forms where we might strictly expect only SAE.

Apparently she does not make a deliberate choice to use BEV. Although her attitude toward BEV is basically positive (Chapter 1), when she read early transcripts of our conversations, she expressed doubt about her use of BEV. She listened to the tapes to confirm this and expressed considerable surprise at hearing herself use so many BEV forms. Furthermore, she showed little awareness of her use of BEV when questioned about it. If we can believe her self-report, her use of BEV came naturally, at least in this situation where she was fairly comfortable and not overly concerned with regulating her speech. For the most part, she was not trying, then, to use BEV to justify her role in a study of BEV. Nor was she trying to avoid BEV because she felt it would stigmatize her. Yet the fact that she thought she was avoiding BEV is striking. She seems to have heard herself playing one role, that of a typical, conforming, college student, while I heard her playing another, that of a BEV speaker.

In writing she usually successfully avoids BEV, perhaps because she is more carefully attending to her language during the act of text production. The more formal and planned Laurie's writing, the better she succeeds in avoiding BEV. In fact, the slip in her note ("you wasn't in") is rare among the samples of her writing I collected. Laurie's desire to come across in the "best" light is somewhat undermined, I believe unconsciously, by her use of BEV in spoken discourse. Rather than contribute to her ethos, as it does with Shanique when she is smart talking, it only detracts from her ladylike image. A "lady" does not use BEV in any context. If Laurie were to condemn BEV wholeheartedly, we could assume that she believes it inappropriate for a lady and that her use of it is attributable to slips of the tongue. But she professes positive feelings about BEV. It may be that she provides an example of a fairly typical phenomenon—the profession of attitudes about speech or writing style that do not match performance.

On Not Talking Back:
African-American Politeness Conventions

Laurie's reliance on language that reinforces her femininity and respectability may be functionally related to her attempt to maintain particular African-American politeness conventions. Specifically, Laurie may be trying to maintain privacy, so valued in African-American culture, by taking on the proper public front. In analyzing Laurie's spoken and written narratives and in examining her self-descriptive statements, I find a continued emphasis on preserving the proper front for the public self. Violation of this norm, a norm so often preserved by females by maintaining silence, is labeled "talking back" by poet Bell Hooks:

> [S]o many black folks have been raised to believe that there is just so much that you should not talk about, not in private and not in public. One of the jokes we used to have about the "got everything" white people is how they just tell all their business, just put their stuff right out there. One point of blackness then became—like how you keep your stuff to yourself, how private you could be about your business. (2)

Kochman, too, discusses the African-American attitude toward divulging personal information. For example, direct questioning about personal business is an affront. The dispensing of personal information is always done at the discretion of the individual involved—not at the request of others:

> Blacks are principally person-oriented. Consequently, what matters first for them are those aspects of self that people actually show in face-to-face interaction: intelligence, wit, charm, sensitivity, or conversely, stupidity, hostility, intolerance, insensitivity, etc. Social information, such as what people do for a living, may never become a topic of conversation in a black social gathering. (*Black and White Styles* 98)

As Kochman goes on to explain, direct questioning about personal information is seen as aggressive—as a way to embarrass someone publicly by asking for or announcing information that would compromise him or her. This is especially so when the interlocutors are not intimate. It may also be seen as hostile—as an attempt to gain information that will be used against one (*Black and White Styles* 98-105). Laurie, then, may be working hard to preserve the proper public front without divulging personal information.

In the case of her letter, she may even be saving face for me by producing a document that can be both public and private without violating African-American politeness conventions. The very artificiality of the situation, that is, the writing of a letter in a classroom setting for a study, may affront her sense of propriety. Foremost among the problems she must solve to maintain equilibrium is the fact that the letter is not really private, yet she must write it as if it were. The text of the letter, which follows, demonstrates how Laurie deals with this conflict between a private self and a public self by drawing on politeness strategies:

Dear Rene,
What's up, honey? I guess you didn't expect to receive a letter from me, seeing that I practically live down the hall. Well, I was required to write a letter to a friend. So after debating for around fifteen minutes I decided to write you.

I don't know if I've ever told you that I'm glad to have you for a friend. So, since I want to give you a few roses while you're alive, I'll tell you now. [Happy face drawn in margin.]

It's nice to have a friend that I can talk to about "mostly" anything. Ha!! Ha!! You know, honey, somethings you just have to keep to yourself.

I think thus far we have had a wonderful freshman year. Seeing that this year is almost over.

We've had enough laughter to last a life time. From going to parties, Greek Shows, talent shows. I don't know how many nights we've spent talking about guys. Especially, when they piss us off or when they do something extra special for us 2 wonderful, sexy, beautiful girls.

I tell you we simply amaze me. Rene, nothing can compare to our college days at UT. I hope that the friendship we have developed lasts forever. And when you bring your spoiled brat over my house, I'm going whip his * * * behind. [Happy face drawn here.]
LOVE YOU ALWAYS SIS,

Laurie
P. S. FRIENDS FOREVER

How does one select a recipient for such a publicly private letter? While Rene is a good choice according to the constraints I had set up (a same-sex, same-race peer), she needs to know why Laurie is writing to her. Laurie attempts to deal with this dilemma by explaining it to Rene; however, she does not fully develop her explanation nor provide quite enough context for Rene. Compare the direct approach taken by Spike and Divinity (Chapter 3). In this respect, Laurie shows herself to be a novice writer, but she also shows that she is attending to another audience (the researcher).

In fact, Laurie has three audiences for this letter:

1. Rene, with whom she has an intimate relationship;
2. the researcher, with whom she has a friendly but formal relationship of unequal power; and
3. the readers of the study, with whom she has a highly abstract and formal relationship.

To meet the constraints of the first audience, she wants to establish her closeness to Rene. In paragraph three she explicitly addresses Rene as a trusted friend with whom she can talk freely. In spoken discourse, she could establish closeness not only by the content of her discourse but also by using BEV, yet in her letter she is restricted because BEV is not a written dialect. As I pointed out in Chapter 1, her use of "honey" in paragraph one and again in paragraph three may draw on BEV, as when "girl" or "chile" often becomes a term of affection or solidarity among women. In this use of "honey" and in the last paragraph, with the hint of a BEV expression ("I'ma whip your black ass" or some variation thereof), she produces a written version of BEV. This is a far cry from the unselfconscious use of BEV in speech. It seems postured to elicit solidarity—and it is restricted to word choice.

Laurie plays to me as the second audience indirectly. For example, while her brief explanation to Rene about why she is writing can be attributed to her lack of writing skill, she also feels that she can later explain the letter to Rene in person. By doing so, she can maintain her sense of propriety, which would require that she not talk about me, while in contrast Spike and Divinity, working from a different agenda, i.e., commenting upon the research, feel free to discuss me directly. My reading is reinforced by the last sentence of paragraph three ("So after debating for around fifteen minutes I decided to write you"), which seems indirectly addressed to me more than it is to Rene. Rene, after all, should have little interest in this background. Instead, she is interested in what Laurie has to say to her. Laurie seems to be letting me in on the process of how she fulfilled the "assignment" required by the study. Because she does not want to jeopardize the integrity of the study by referring directly to it, she resorts to indirection.

As regards the third audience, the eventual readers of the study, Laurie's main task is to preserve the proper public front, to appear ladylike and respectable. Thus, we see a tension between what can and what cannot be said "in public." By making the letter serve a phatic function, a reaffirmation of her friendship with Rene, Laurie meets the demands of a public performance that does not reveal too much personal information and solves the problem of what to say to someone she sees frequently. This is expressed quite directly in paragraph two ("I don't know if I've ever told you I'm glad to have you for a friend").

Laurie's letter specifically constructs a ladylike ethos in other ways besides maintaining a decorous silence about me as a reader or about the role of this letter in a study. In paragraph two, she displays a sunny disposition and a tendency to accentuate the positive. The expression "Give you a few roses" and the happy face drawings show her as optimistic and positive. Her direct statement of friendship in paragraph three ("It's nice to have a friend that I can talk to about 'mostly' anything") is engaging and complimentary, calculated to make the reader feel good and to recognize that the writer values her.

The quotes around "mostly" seem to demand some comment. They may indicate a colloquial use of "almost," showing that Laurie sees anything except formal academic prose as deviate. But the quotes may also indicate emphasis—making her point that there are limits to even the best friendships. Such a reading reinforces the conjecture that Laurie is aware of a conflict between the public/private nature of this letter. Her next sentence ("Ha!! Ha!! You know, honey, somethings you just have to keep to yourself") suggests a possible inside joke. As friends, Laurie and Rene have secrets that others (the researcher or other readers) cannot be allowed to share. Notice that at this point, where Laurie is at least by implication drawing boundaries between herself and Rene (and perhaps between the two friends and the outside researcher), the friendly BEV expression "honey" comes into play. By reinforcing her closeness to Rene, BEV supports that aspect of her ladylike ethos that requires her to accentuate the positive and be supportive of others.

Laurie accentuates the positive again in paragraph four ("I think thus far we have had a wonderful freshman year"). She seems to be cheering on Rene (and herself), implying "we've almost made it through." But the cheerleader suddenly gets earthy: "I don't know how many nights we've spent talking about guys. Especially, when they piss us off or when they do something extra special for us 2 wonderful, sexy, beautiful girls." "Piss us off" is frank and not ladylike. Again the phrase seems to be a move for solidarity, since it shows that Rene is privileged to hear Laurie in her most informal persona. Yet even in this instance decorum is important, for Laurie's use of "piss us off" takes place in an appropriate context, that is, in addressing a close friend informally and personally.

Anxious to preserve a feminine ethos and to show solidarity with Rene, Laurie comments about "guys" and about her and Rene's beauty. Her humor, although obvious, is not self-deprecating. She plays the cheerleader again, or at least the typical college co-ed, with all the typical concerns, and has moved into a humorous, self-congratulatory tone ("we simply amaze me"). Throughout this final paragraph, she reaffirms the purpose of the letter. As I elsewhere noted (Chapter 1), she transforms, and this time cleans up, a phrase commonly used by BEV speakers: "I'ma whip your black ass" becomes "I'm going whip his * * * behind."

My detailed reading of Laurie's letter is meant to illustrate her functional use of superpoliteness strategies. Superpoliteness allows her a way to maintain the proper distinction between a private and a public self. In the letter she pursues a conciliatory agenda—to establish a closer personal bond and to take on the role of enabler, of a cheerleader who accentuates the positive in order to help both herself and her ostensible reader face the difficulties of college life. But she also establishes the proper tone for a public/personal letter. She discloses nothing personal about herself or Rene, says nothing that would violate African-American politeness norms, at the same time giving me, the researcher, what I want.

Her other discourse forms, both spoken and written, show a similar concern for ladylike behavior and the proper public front as well as a similar use of superpolite forms. Comparisons between the written and spoken versions of her narrative and persuasive discourse reveals a consistent though sometimes slightly different attempt to preserve decorum. The written version of her narrative, for example, portrays her as more concerned with appearance and more bold than the spoken. Thus, with more time for reflection and careful attention to language, Laurie increases the level of superpoliteness.

The earlier version of the narrative was the spoken, presented below:

> But I know one thing that happened to me. Well I can laugh now but at the time it wasn't that funny. . . . I have these boots and they're real slippery. So I was about to go home one weekend, this is just this past weekend. And me and my roommate was walking 'cause I had, I had to walk over to Jester [a dormitory] to meet a friend. So my roommate was helping me; I didn't have that many bags at all. So my roommate was helping me carry a bag, and, uh, she had on her, uh, some tennies. And it had been raining real bad that day. So she say, "Come on, Laurie, let's go down this hill 'cause I want to make you fall." And I said, "No, I'm not going down that hill because I'm not going to fall." And this, uh, but for some stupid reason I went anyway. (*hits desk for emphasis*) I said, I said, "OK but look, this is how I'll walk so I won't fall." And I was doing the, trying to walk real slow and I was walking hard. And the next thing I knew I was just down! (*Valerie laughs*) I mean I was on my back! And I was so embarrassed, and she helped me up and I mean even though she had said she had wanted me to fall, you know, it was like, I didn't really expect for you to fall. And then so I tried to blame it on her, you know, like, I say "You wanted me to fall, chile, you wanted me to fall!" (*Valerie laughing*) Like, but then I looked and it wasn't, it wasn't hardly anybody around, so I was glad about that. She said, "Well nobody didn't see you."

This story illustrates a "fall from pride" theme, and is thus directly concerned with maintaining face publicly in light of an embarrassing situation. Although she knows better, Laurie believes she can get down the hill safely by controlling her walk. She ends up in a ridiculous prone position, casting about for someone to blame yet realizing it was her own fault for overstepping her boundaries. In the end, it is humiliation that gets the focus. Her main concern is whether or not anyone has seen her. Her public front must be maintained.

The written version of this story adds a few illuminating details, particularly those about her appearance. By describing herself as well-dressed, she emphasizes the importance of her front.

The Day I Fell

About a month ago, my room-mate and I were walking to Jester [a dormitory]. The rain had been coming down hard and the roads were slippery. Yet, I did not mind, because I was happy that I was going home for the weekend. Rain, sleet or snow, nothing was going to stop me from going home.

Anyway, I had on some dressy clothes and my leather boots. Because, I wanted my momma to think I had been taking good care of myself and to be extra proud of me. My room-mate was carrying one bag for me and I was carrying two. We were almost at Jester when my room-mate started walking down this ramp. So I said that I wasn't going that way. She then said, "Come on down, because I want you to fall." If you know me you'd know that I'm a bold person. Therefore, I was determined to walk down that ramp without falling. So I started walking extra hard and at the same time I was saying, this is how I walk so I won't fall. When all of a sudden, I fell. This was not an ordinary slip. No, instead I fell flat on my back.

Consequently, I was very embarrassed. All I could think of was who saw me. When I saw there were no cute Black guys around, I jumped up. My back wasn't hurt, just my pride. Thankfully, my room-mate did not laugh. At least not in my face, but I'm sure she did after I left. You know I think I'll ask her today. Then again who cares—We all have our embarassing moments and that just happened to be one of mine.

Appearance is explicitly mentioned as important and is described in more detail ("dressy clothes" and "leather boots") than in the spoken version. In going home, she hopes to prove by her appearance that she is capable and mature. She also maintains the same positive outlook we see in her letter. For example, she portrays herself as happy about going home for the weekend and unperturbed by the dismal weather.

There is a surprising change in Laurie's self-description in the written narrative. She overtly states that she is a "bold," that is, a brave, person. The walk down the ramp (changed from a hill) takes on the character of a challenge. Almost like Don Quixote, Laurie sets herself up to conquer the ramp. In this version she also specifies exactly for whom she wants to preserve her front—"cute Black guys." Finally, her roommate is portrayed as more polite, but less reassuring. While in the spoken version she is an insider who participates in the "joke," in the written version she is another person for whom Laurie must preserve a front.

The ending should not surprise any teacher of composition. It resorts to the fairly common device of novice writers, the tacked-on moral ("We all have our embarassing moments and that just happened to be one of mine"). The moral supports the view of the narrative as a "fall of pride" tale and seems to allow Laurie to conform to her view of academic essays. It further enhances her ethos as a lady, for it illustrates her willingness to abide by social norms (eschewing excessive pride) and to stay humbly in her place.

Laurie, then, contends with two problems in speaking and one in writing. Her speaking reveals not only attention to those ladylike qualities that can undermine her power, but it also draws upon her first dialect, BEV. Her writing, although conforming to SAE, conforms also to the superpolite forms that put her in a double bind. Thus, while she intends to construct a ladylike ethos that will garner her respect—probably an image she sees as appropriate to an educated person—her interlocutors may construct an ethos for her that puts her in an inferior position, especially intellectually. Consider again her letter. Her accentuation of the positive and her stress on creating solidarity and maintaining African-American politeness conventions prompt her to ignore using the letter for the stereotypically more "serious" business of delivering news. Consider again her narrative. Her stress on appearance and on how others will view her makes her seem shallow and leaves her with a rather conventional moral. Finally, her indirect criticism of sororities and her unwillingness to appear aggressive mark her argument as less than committed (a comment also made about Shanique's written argument).

Who fares better? Shanique, who seems so unconcerned with being ladylike and so intent on being independent that she ignores politeness and even appears cruel? Or Laurie, who is so concerned with being ladylike that her credibility as an intellectual suffers? If pressed to choose, I would say that Shanique's energy and assertiveness will gain for her more power than Laurie's superpoliteness. Yet neither fares well enough. In the world of academic prose, with its grounding in masculine and European traditions of discourse, not only Laurie but also Shanique and Max and Polo and Thomas are at a decided disadvantage.

Cultural Diversity in Rhetorical Study

Before presenting my own conclusions, I want to give voice to my informants. I asked them to read and respond to drafts of my original analysis of their talk and writing and was quite surprised but also encouraged by the degree to which they accepted the task. Not only did they confirm much of my interpretation, but their helpful comments also guided my subsequent readings of their texts.

The Students Comment

Max wrote no comments, prompting me to call him (since he was out of town) for more information. Over the phone he said he was satisfied with the analysis. I sensed he was a bit uneasy, and he confirmed that he felt awkward reading about himself. His writing sometimes sounded "bloated," he said, although he had been unaware of that effect of his style. I explained to him that the effect depended to a large degree on the audience and asked him if he would change his style at this point. He answered that he would be more careful, that he would take more time and think more about how his audience might receive his words. I asked him if he was aware of the tradition of fancy talk; he was very much aware of it, especially, but not exclusively, in a romantic context. As he said, he was conscious of fancy talk being used in a number of persuasive situations. He was quick to tell me that he had never intended in his essays to "manipulate" the audience in a sinister way. Nor was he consciously trying to sound intelligent, but just trying to sound his best. (My claim is that in trying to do his best he picked a style that he stereotypically associates with academic English and that would thus make him sound intelligent.)

After talking to Max, I was, and I remain, somewhat disturbed by the possible personal effects of this research on his concept of his own writing. His use of the term "bloated" was certainly more negative than I would have wished. In fact, during the writing of this book, I have seen many more positive aspects of Max's use of African-American rhetoric—his artistry and adventurousness strike me more forcefully now than they ever have. Max also told me he had decided to study divinity and become a preacher—evidence, I think, that he values his verbal ability.

Like Max, Shanique wrote almost no comments on the manuscript; however, she did discuss the analysis with me, in a final, untaped interview. Most of our discussion was initiated by my questions, since she cautiously claimed to have no problems with what she had read and no points of disagreement. She did note in writing that she had at first been surprised by the transcripts of her speech and that she had felt "the dialogue sounded like the stereotypical, illiterate Black man." But listening to the tape made her realize that the difference was actually one between speaking and writing and that "it didn't sound as bad as it looked." I think this is interesting in the light of Shanique's avoidance of BEV in her writing. It confirms my sense that she feels that BEV is highly inappropriate in writing but not necessarily in speaking. Furthermore, her surprise about how she sounds on the tapes confirms my belief that she uses BEV somewhat unselfconsciously in casual speech.

Had she consciously tried to present herself as mean, in other words, as independent, and tough? She agreed that she had done so, although she had thought of herself as coming off more as independent than tough. Had BEV contributed to her ethos? According to Shanique, it did help her communicate the image she had aimed for, but she explained that she expected her listeners to understand BEV for her to try this strategy. This seems to contradict her use of BEV with me unless it is remembered that she considered me knowledgeable about BEV. BEV has always promoted her independent image, and she naturally relies on it when that is the ethos she wishes to construct and she believes the audience will be receptive.

I was not surprised when Shanique confessed to changing her stories for effect, though she explained that she did not change the truth but simply embellished it. For example, she actually set the cat on fire, as she claims in the spoken version of her story about her grandmother's farm, and she did not put it in the wood burning stove, as the written version claims. However, her aunt had burned a cat in a stove as a child (at least according to family legend), and Shanique had chosen this twist to the story for the written version for reasons of economy.

At the time of this interview, Shanique had just finished an advanced expository writing class in which her instructor encouraged her to develop her voice by attending to her spoken language. Like me, he found some of her more formal writing less exciting than her informal (according to Shanique, less "boring," although I doubt he put it exactly that way). Asked how she would change her writing style, Shanique reported she would probably use more dialogue in the narrative and try to keep the "tone" of her storytelling in all her writing. (I believe she means by "tone" what writing teachers mean by "voice.") When I asked Shanique how she would keep the "tone" of her speaking and still write acceptable academic prose, she was at a loss for specific answers. I suggested prewriting in her natural dialect, whether BEV or SAE, whatever seemed right, imagining she was speaking to a friendly listener, then editing for correctness and coherence. I also suggested that in reading she pay attention to how the author uses strategies similar to her own to tell a good story. These are perhaps simplistic remedies, but I am sure they are on the right track for her case. And they are remedies she can work on independently.

I also had feedback from Laurie, Dinese, and Divinity. Dinese had very little to say, other than that she basically agreed with my analysis. As I have mentioned in Chapter 3, she has a strong feeling that BEV and SAE are not different dialects, and she reconfirmed that feeling in her comments. For Dinese, BEV is marked only by lexicon and pronunciation. Grammar is identical to that of other nonstandard (and incorrect) dialects of SAE, i.e., rural and Southern. From her point of view, singling out BEV as a separate dialect comes from the impulse to attach social stigmas to African-Americans.

Laurie did not provide written comments but did speak to me on the phone. Her only point of concern was my claim that Shanique, her close friend, uses BEV consciously in speaking to construct a "mean" ethos. Remember, however, that although Shanique said she did not really think of herself as coming across as mean, she did use BEV, more or less deliberately to show herself as independent. Perhaps "strong" would be a better word than mean or tough. Laurie made the point, which I believe is crucial and correct in relation to most of Shanique's speech, that she and Shanique do not consciously employ BEV but that it simply comes naturally to them. When I asked her why it does not occur in her writing she explained that because of the way she learned to write and because of her extensive reading, she naturally excludes BEV from written discourse. This may be the most important lesson we can learn from a BEV speaker who is also a successful student. It underscores the fact that BEV and SAE are separate styles with separate domains. Laurie may have learned so well to conform to SAE in writing because of exceptional character, higher than average intelligence, or a favorable personal environment, advantages many students do not enjoy.

Divinity, whom, I admit, I expected to be rather critical because of her signifying essay, made some helpful comments about the manuscript (an unclear sentence, for example), and provided very useful feedback about fancy talk, which she recognized as a register preachers often employ: "Preachers do a lot of '[fancy] talk.' What a study THAT would be!" Perhaps being true to her chosen profession as a writer, she even parodied fancy talk for me in her comments:

> I ain't even read the whole thing. But, based upon presumptive evidence on the part of this student it would behoove me if I were not granted the most superlative superlative privilege of extending my warmest regards and signatures to whatever paper necessary to grant the aforementioned Doctoral candidate her Doctorate. That talk about [fancy] talk has started something in *this* writer's mind!

Besides commenting on fancy talk, Divinity expressed some doubt about Thomas' claim that he learned BEV as a second dialect, telling me that perhaps he was "pullin' yo' leg." However, she does not offer clear evidence of this; it is simply a suspicion on her part. She also mentions her respect for Shanique's storytelling ability, warning me again not to take the stories as Gospel: "I love Shanique's Ethos or whatever. But, she tells stories so well that I sometimes wonder if the stories are 'true word for word.'" Divinity is pointing out to me, in case as an outsider I have missed it, the tendency toward hyperbole that good African-American storytellers are expected to employ. It is quite interesting that at this stage in our relationship she has foregone signifying for a more direct commentary. My request for direct commentary elicited just that.

Conclusions

The viewpoints of speakers and writers, when available, are among the many sources we should consult when analyzing and interpreting texts from a cultural perspective. The production of texts is influenced by a writer's linguistic background and cultural heritage. Thus, awareness of the needs, goals, and perceptions of writers is an essential component of a sensitive rhetorical inter-pretation. Likewise, we must consult, with a critical eye and a knowledge of the current state of knowledge, the scholarly litera-ture on the cultural group to which the writer belongs. Acquain-tance with relevant literary traditions and texts can enrich rhetorical analyses as well. In all cases, careful consideration should be given to the viewpoints of scholars belonging to the group under study—in this particular instance the testimony of African-American linguists like Mitchell-Kernan and Baugh carry great weight.

Without a knowledge of African-American rhetoric, I could not have adequately analyzed these texts. This is most vividly illustrated in the case of Divinity, whose signifying on my research so baffled me when I first encountered in her narrative essay her suggestion that I might be, since I was asking her to write about a time she broke a rule or broke the law, a "white less bigoted than a Klansman but bigoted nonetheless." My first read-ing of this text caused me dismay; I immediately assumed she was expressing anger. After a great deal of reading about African-American politeness conventions and rhetorical strategies, I was able to revise that reading to reconcile the text with Divinity's obvious friendly demeanor toward me. My revised reading recog-nized her statement as signifying, a polite way of notifying me that African-Americans are not to be defined by deviance. Her indirectness was appropriate as a rhetorical strategy, for it allowed her to deal with a superior without direct challenge. As far as Divinity was concerned, if the shoe fit, I would wear it. Similarly, my understanding of signifying, fancy talk, respectable talk, and mean talk allowed me to read these texts with a sharper eye and a better understanding of what effects the writers were striving to achieve.

Just as a knowledge of the workings of African-American language and rhetoric contribute to a reading of these texts, the texts themselves illuminate and illustrate the findings of other scholars interested in BEV. We see, for example, how attitudes toward BEV, both negative and positive, have made these writers self-conscious about their language. In turn, this self-consciousness has to be contended with when they write. They generally display ambiguity about BEV—seeing it simultaneously as "uneducated" or "bad English" and as "poetic" or a mark of group solidarity and identity. Thus, they are often at a loss as to how and when to use BEV in the university setting. But they find ways to negotiate this dilemma. One ingenious strategy they employ is to associate BEV with "slang," by which they seem to mean, roughly, informal language appropriate for peers. By using versions of this slang in their letters, the most informal of their writing, they create a sense of solidarity with their readers. Unfortunately, they do not often employ such tactics in their academic writing. Shanique's decision to exclude BEV from her narratives is the most extreme example of how a writer can be left without appropriate rhetorical strategies when a major means of expression is denied.

Blanket negative attitudes toward BEV on the part of educators is harmful to these students' sense of identity. It is painful to hear Polo call BEV "improper" and to hear his stories of correcting his friends' English, for one can only imagine their hostile reaction as he thus removes himself from their world. And Thomas portrays himself in these texts as the perennial outsider, not comfortable with BEV yet not accepted by many of his white peers at the university in spite of his mastery of SAE. Ironically, Thomas himself is unaware that his academically oriented writing bears some hallmarks of African-American rhetoric. Yet his academic writing clearly employs fancy talk strategies in its reliance on impressive "big" words and its dramatic flair.

The richness of the African-American rhetorical tradition has been ignored for too long by teachers and students of academic writing. The fancy talk tradition, which many African-American students will undoubtedly recognize from its street versions, has a long history, respectable as well as roguish. We can castigate this tradition and alienate young African-Americans from appreciating it, or we can celebrate it, expose all students to it, regardless of their racial or ethnic background, explore its rhetorical employment of hyperbole, amplification, parallelism, and playfulness. Certainly, the African-American preacher's art, thanks to orators such as Martin Luther King, Jr., is afforded some measure of attention and respect in college writing classes, yet, considering the scope of African-American rhetoric, this seems but a token. Tea meeting speeches, ring play songs and jump rope rhymes, prayers, rifting, fancy talking, signifying, and modern-day rapping are other legitimate and influential verbal art forms that could profitably be studied in the writing classroom. An emphasis on African-American rhetoric would be an opportunity to expand and enrich our academic discourse that, under a paradigm of white, middle-class, male domination, has traded flexibility for stability and has thus become more rigid than it need be.

Bibliography

Abrahams, Roger D. *Deep Down in the Jungle: Negro Narrative Folklore from the Streets of Philadelphia.* 1st rev. ed. 1963. Chicago: Aldine Publishing Co., 1970.

———. *Positively Black.* Englewood Cliffs, NJ: Prentice Hall, 1970.

———. "The Training of the Man-of-Words in Talking Sweet." *Language in Society.* 1 (1972): 15–29.

———. "Black Talking on the Streets." *Explorations in the Ethnography of Speaking.* Eds. Richard Bauman and Joel Sherzer. London: Cambridge University Press, 1974. 240–62.

———. "Negotiating Respect: Patterns of Presentation among Black Women." *Journal of American Folklore* 88 (1975): 58–80.

———. *Talking Black.* Rowley, MA: Newbury House, 1976.

———. *The Man-of-Words in the West Indies: Performance and the Emergence of Creole Culture.* Baltimore and London: The Johns Hopkins University Press, 1983.

———, ed. *Afro-American Folktales: Stories from Black Traditions in the New World.* New York: Pantheon Books, 1985.

Agar, Michael H. *Speaking of Ethnography.* Qualitative Research Methods. Vol. 2. Beverly Hills, New York, New Delhi: Sage Publications, 1986.

Angelou, Maya. *I Know Why the Caged Bird Sings.* New York: Bantam Books, 1971.

Bartholomae, David. "Inventing the University." *When a Writer Can't Write: Studies in Writer's Block and Other Composing Process Problems.* Ed. Mike Rose. New York and London: Guilford Press, 1985.

Baugh, John. *Black Street Speech: Its History, Structure, and Survival.* Austin: The University of Texas Press, 1983.

Beaman, Karen. "Coordination and Subordination Revisited: Syntactic Complexity in Spoken and Written Narrative Discourse." In Tannen: 1984. 45–80.

Berger, Peter, and Thomas Luckman. *The Social Construction of Reality.* New York: Doubleday, 1967.

Bentley, Robert H. "Social Dialects: Educational Implications of the Study of Black English." In *The Legacy of Language: A Tribute to Charlton Laird.* Ed. Philip C. Boardman. Reno and Las Vegas: University of Nevada Press, 1987. 69–80.

Blom, Jan-Petter, and John J. Gumperz. "Social Meaning in Linguistic Structure: Code-switching in Norway." Eds. John J. Gumperz and Dell Hymes. *Directions in Sociolinguistics: The Ethnography of Communication.* New York: Holt, Rinehart, and Winston, 1972. 407–434.

Britton, James, Tony Burgess, Nancy Martin, Alex McLeod, and Harold Rosen. *The Development of Writing Abilities* (11–18). 1975. London: Macmillan, 1977.

Canuteson, Mary Alice. "A Perceptual Study of English Teachers and Language Arts Supervisors Concerning the Use of Vernacular Black English by Students and Teachers in the State of Texas." Diss. University of North Texas, 1982.

Chafe, Wallace L. "Integration and Involvement in Speaking, Writing, and Oral Literature." In Tannen, 1982. 34–54.

Coates, Jennifer. *Women, Men and Language: A Sociolinguistic Account of Sex Differences in Language.* London and New York: Longman, 1986.

Crane, Stephen. *The Portable Stephen Crane.* New York and London: Penguin Books, 1969.

Dance, Daryl Cumber. *Shuckin' and Jivin': Folklore from Contemporary Black Americans.* Bloomington and London: Indiana University Press, 1978.

Davis, Gerald L. *I Got the Word in Me and I Can Sing It, You Know: A Study of the Performed African-American Sermon.* Philadelphia: University of Pennsylvania Press, 1985.

Dillard, J. L. *Black English: Its History and Usage in the United States.* New York: Random House, 1972.

Dundes, Alan, ed. *Mother Wit from the Laughing Barrel: Readings in the Interpretation of Afro-American Folklore.* Englewood Cliffs, NJ: Prentice-Hall, 1973.

Erickson, Frederick. "Rhetoric, Anecdote, and Rhapsody: Coherence Strategies in a Conversation Among Black American Adolescents." In Tannen, 1984. 81–154.

Fine, Michelle. "Silencing in Public Schools." *Language Arts* 64.2 (February 1987): 157–74.

Fordham, Signithia, and John U. Ogbu. "Black Students' School Success: Coping with the 'Burden of Acting White.'" *Urban Review* 18.3 (1986): 176–206.

Fordham, Signithia. "Racelessness as a Factor in Black Students' School Success: Pragmatic Strategy or Pyrrhic Victory?" *Harvard Educational Review* 58.1 (February 1988): 54–84.

Foster, Michele. "'It's Cookin' Now': A Performance Analysis of the Speech Events of a Black Teacher in an Urban Community College." *Language in Society* 18 (1989): 1–29.

Fowler, H. Ramsey, and Jane A. Aaron. *The Little, Brown Handbook.* 4th ed. Glenview, IL: Scott, Foresman and Co., 1989.

Fraser, Bruce. "Some 'Unexpected' Reactions to Various American-English Dialects." Shuy and Fasold, 1973. 28–40.

Garner, T., and D. L. Rubin. "Middle Class Black Perceptions of Dialect and Style Shifting: The Case of Southern Attorneys." *Journal of Language and Social Psychology* 5.1 (1986): 33–48.

Gates, Henry Louis, Jr. *The Signifying Monkey: A Theory of African American Literary Criticism.* New York and Oxford: Oxford University Press, 1988.

Gere, Anne Ruggles. "A Cultural Perspective on Talking and Writing." Kroll and Vann, 1981. 11–123.

Goffman, Erving. *The Presentation of Self in Everyday Life.* Garden City, NY: Doubleday Anchor Books, 1959.

Goss, Linda, and Marian E. Barnes, eds. *Talk That Talk: An Anthology of African American Storytelling.* New York: Simon and Schuster, 1989.

Gregory, Michael, and Susanne Carroll. *Language and Situation: Language Varieties and Their Social Contexts.* Boston: Routledge & Kegan Paul, 1978.

Gumperz, J. "The Speech Community." In *Language and Social Context.* Ed. Pier Paolo Giglioli. 1972. Harmondsworth, England: Penguin Books, 1980. 219–31.

Hancock, Ian. "Identity, Equality, and Standard Language." *The Florida FL Reporter* (Spring/Fall 1974): 49–52, 101–03.

———. "A Preliminary Classification of the Anglophone Atlantic Creoles with Syntactic Data from Thirty-Three Representative Dialects." In *Pidgin and Creole Languages: Essays in Memory of John E. Reinecke.* Ed. G. G. Gilbert. New York: Cambridge University Press, 1980. 264–333.

Hannerz, Ulf. *Soulside.* New York and London: Columbia University Press, 1969.

Heath, Shirley Brice. "Protean Shapes in Literacy Events: Evershifting Oral and Literate Traditions." In Tannen, 1982. 91–118.

———. *Ways with Words: Language, Life, and Work in Communities and Classrooms.* New York: Cambridge University Press, 1983.

Hill, Alette Olin. *Mother Tongue, Father Time: A Decade of Linguistic Revolt.* Bloomington: Indiana University Press, 1986.

Hooks, Bell. *Talking Back: Thinking Feminist, Thinking Black.* Boston: South End Press, 1989.

Hurston, Zora Neale. *Mules and Men.* 1935. Bloomington: Indiana University Press, 1978.

Hymes, Dell. *Foundations in Sociolinguistics.* Philadelphia: University of Pennsylvania Press, 1974.

Ingraham, J. H. *The Southwest by a Yankee.* 1835. Vol. II. Ann Arbor, Michigan: University Microfilms, 1966.

Irmscher, William F. "Finding a Comfortable Identity." *College Composition and Communication* 38: (February 1987): 81–87.

Johnson, James Weldon. *God's Trombones: Seven Negro Sermons in Verse.* 1927. New York: Viking Press, 1969.

Joiner, Charles C. *Memorandum and Opinion*: 7–71861. *Black English and the Education of Black Children and Youth.* Ed. Geneva Smitherman. Detroit: Center for Black Studies, 1981.

Jones, Bessie and Bess Lomax Hawes. *Step It Down: Games, Plays, Song, and Stories from the Afro-American Heritage*. New York: Harper and Row, 1972.

Jones, Rachel L. "What's Wrong With Black English?" *Newsweek* 100 (December 27, 1982): 7.

Jones-Jackson, Patricia. "Oral Tradition of Prayer in Gullah." *The Journal of Religious Thought* 39 (1982): 21–33.

Kerr-Mattox, Beverly. "Language Attitudes of Teachers and Prospective Teachers Toward Black and White Speakers." Masters Thesis. Texas A&M University, 1989.

Kochman, Thomas. *Rappin' and Stylin' Out: Communication in Urban Black America*. Urbana, Chicago, and London: University of Illinois Press, 1972.

———. "Strategic Ambiguity in Black Speech Genres: Cross-Cultural Interference in Participant-Observation Research." Text 6.2 (1986): 153–70.

———. *Black and White Styles in Conflict*. Chicago and London: The University of Chicago Press, 1981.

Kroll, Barry M., and Roberta J. Vann, eds. *Exploring Speaking-Writing Relationships: Connections and Contrasts*. Urbana, IL: NCTE, 1981.

Labov, William, Paul Cohen, Clarence Robins, and John Lewis. *A Study of the Nonstandard English of Negro and Puerto Rican Speakers in New York City*. Report on Co-operative Research Project 3288. Vols. I and II. New York: Columbia University, 1968.

Labov, William. *The Social Stratification of English in New York City*. Washington, DC: Center for Applied Linguistics, 1966.

———. *The Study of Nonstandard English*. Champaign, IL: National Council of Teachers of English, 1970.

———. "The Logic of Nonstandard English." *Language in the Inner City*. Philadelphia: University of Pennsylvania Press, 1972.

———. *Sociolinguistic Patterns*. Philadelphia: University of Pennsylvania Press, 1973.

Ladner, Caryle, and Ossie Guffy. *The Autobiography of a Black Woman*. New York: Norton, 1971.

Lakoff, Robin. *Language and Women's Place*. New York: Harper and Row, 1975.

———. "Some of My Favorite Writers Are Literate: The Mingling of Oral and Literate Strategies in Written Communication." In Tannen, 1982. 239–60.

Le Page, R. B., and Andrée Tabouret-Keller. *Acts of Identity: Creole-based Approaches to Language and Ethnicity*. Cambridge: Cambridge University Press, 1985.

Lynch, Louis. *The Barbados Book*. London: Andre Deutsch, 1964.

Mays, Luberta. *Black Children's Perception of the Use of Their Dialect*. San Francisco: R & E Research Associates, Inc., 1977.

Michaels, Sarah, and James Collins. "Oral Discourse Styles: Classroom Interaction and the Acquisition of Literacy." In Tannen, 1984. 219–44.

Mitchell-Kernan, Claudia. *Language Behavior in a Black Urban Community*. Language-Behavior Research Laboratory. Working Paper Number 23. University of California, Berkeley. October 1969.

———. "Signifying and Marking: Two Afro-American Speech Acts." In *Directions in Sociolinguistics: The Ethnography of Communication*. Eds. John J. Gumperz and Dell Hymes. New York: Holt, Rinehart and Winston, 1972.

Mulderig, Gerald P., and Langdon Elsbree. *The Heath Handbook*. 12th. ed. Lexington, MA and Toronto: D. C. Heath and Company, 1990.

O'Barr, William M., and Bowman K. Atkins. "'Women's Language' or 'Powerless Language'?" In *Women and Language in Literature and Society*. Eds. Sally McConnell-Ginet, Ruth Borker, and Nelly Furman. New York: Praeger, 1980. 93-110.

O'Keefe, Barbara J. "Writing, Speaking, and the Production of Discourse." Kroll and Vann, 1981. 134–41.

Olson, David R. "From Utterance to Text: The Bias of Language in Speech and Writing." *Harvard Educational Review* 47 (1977): 257–81.

———. "Writing: The Divorce of the Author from the Text." In Kroll and Vann, 1981. 99–110.

Piché, Gene L., Donald L. Rubin, et al. "Teachers' Subjective Evaluations of Standard and Black Nonstandard English Compositions: A Study of Written Language and Attitudes." *Research in the Teaching of English* 12.2 (1978): 107–118.

Pipes, William H. *Say Amen, Brother! Old-Time Negro Preaching: A Study in American Frustration.* Westport, CT: Negro Universities Press, 1951.

Pitts, Walter. "Linguistic Variation as a Function of Ritual Frames in the Afro-Baptist Church in Central Texas." Diss. The University of Texas at Austin, 1986.

Rosenberg, Bruce A. *The Art of the American Folk Preacher.* New York: Oxford University Press, 1970.

Saville-Troike, Muriel. *The Ethnography of Communication: An Introduction.* Oxford: Basil Blackwell, 1982.

Scott, Jerrie. "Mixed Dialects in the Composition Classroom." In *Language Variety in the South.* Eds. Michael B. Montgomery and Guy Bailey. Tuscaloosa: The University of Alabama Press, 1986. 332–47.

Seligman, C. R., G. R. Tucker, and W. E. Lambert. "The Effects of Speech Style and Other Attributes on Teachers' Attitudes Towards Pupils." *Language In Society* 1 (1972): 131–42.

Shafer, John C. "The Linguistic Analysis of Spoken and Written Texts." In Kroll and Vann, 1981. 1–31.

Shaughnessy, Mina P. *Errors and Expectations.* New York: Oxford University Press, 1977.

Shuy, Roger W., and Ralph W. Fasold, eds. *Language Attitudes: Current Trends and Prospects.* Washington, DC: Georgetown University Press, 1973.

Shuy, Roger W., and Frederick Williams. "Stereotyped Attitudes of Selected English Dialect Communities." In Shuy and Fasold, 1973. 85–96.

Sledd, James. "In Defense of the Students' Right." *College English* 45 (November 1983): 667–75.

Smitherman, Geneva. *Talkin' and Testifyin' The Language of Black America.* Boston: Houghton Mifflin, 1977.

Smitherman-Donaldson, Geneva. 1987. "Toward a National Public Policy on Language." *College English* 40 (1977): 30–36.

Sonntag, Selma K., and Jonathan Pool. "Linguistic Denial and Linguistic Self-Denial: American Ideologies of Language." *Language Problems and Language Planning.* 11.1 (Spring 1987): 46–65.

Tannen, Deborah. "A Comparative Analysis of Oral Narrative Strategies: Athenian Greek and American English." In *The Pear Stories: Cognitive, Cultural, and Linguistic Aspects of Narrative Production.* Ed. Wallace L. Chafe. Norwood, NJ: Ablex, 1980. 51–88.

———, ed. *Spoken and Written Language: Exploring Orality and Literacy.* Norwood, NJ: Ablex, 1982.

———. "The Oral/Literate Continuum in Discourse." In Tannen, 1982. 1–16.

———, ed. *Cohesion in Spoken and Written Discourse.* Norwood, NJ: Ablex, 1984.

———. "Spoken and Written Narrative in English and Greek." In Tannen, 1984. 21–44.

Trudgill, Peter. "Acts of Identity: The Sociolinguistics of British Pop-song Pronunciation." *On Dialect: Social and Geographical Perspectives.* Oxford: Basil Blackwell, 1983. 141–60.

Tucker, G. R., and W. E. Lambert. "White and Negro Listeners' Reactions to Various American-English Dialects." *Social Forces* 47 (1969): 464–68.

Wideman, John Edgar. *Brothers and Keepers.* New York: Penguin Books, 1984.

Williams, Frederick. "Some Research Notes on Dialect Attitudes and Stereotypes." In Shuy and Fasold, 1973. 113–128.